MW00830712

JAPANESE AMERICAN
BASEBALL *in California*

A HISTORY

KERRY YO NAKAGAWA

Charleston   London

THE
History
PRESS

Published by The History Press
Charleston, SC 29403
www.historypress.net

Copyright © 2014 by Kerry Yo Nakagawa
All rights reserved

First published 2014

Manufactured in the United States

ISBN 978.1.62619.582.0

Library of Congress CIP data applied for.

To my mama, Yoshiko Rose Nakagawa, who shared that Family, Food, Faith and "True Friends" are the essentials of life and that you should always be proud of your Royal Samurai roots.

CONTENTS

ACKNOWLEDGEMENTS

To keep the flow of goodness coming, always be thankful.
—Nakagawa proverb

I remember walking down my hallway as a child and looking up to see the photo of my uncle Johnny standing next to Lou Gehrig, Kenichi Zenimura and Babe Ruth. I asked him once about the photo, and he modestly said, "I was on Lou Gehrig's team, and we beat Babe Ruth's team 13–3." When I began coaching my son, Kale, and Brandon Zenimura as Little League all-stars, I realized that two generations had gone by since the Nakagawa and Zenimura families had first shared the baseball diamond. I knew these two young all-stars had no knowledge of the unique bond shared by our family baseball history. I immediately began a quest to record data, acquire photos and artifacts and conduct oral histories. Starting with my own family, and then reaching out to many others, I gathered the history from the pioneers, who were now in their eighties and nineties. The Nisei generation is almost gone now, but their efforts, sacrifices and courage will never be forgotten. This missing chapter and hidden legacy that was part of American baseball history led to the creation of the Nisei Baseball Research Project (NBRP), a nonprofit organization that has given us an opportunity to honor our heroes and to bring awareness and education about Japanese American concentration camps through the prism of baseball and our multimedia projects.

In 2001, our book, *Through a Diamond: 100 Years of Japanese American Baseball*, was born. This presentation would not have existed without the generosity of George and Sakaye Aratani and my childhood swim team coach of the Fowler Flippers, John G. Goode of Davis Skaggs Investment Management of San Francisco. Our publisher, Terri Boekhoff, was our guardian angel, and she and her peers walked me through many labor-intense hours and believed in our fascinating history. A Hall of Fame thanks to Tom Seaver for contributing the foreword and putting Fresno and California on the map with his athleticism and humanity. *Arigatos* and hugs in spirit to my godpapa Noriyuki "Pat" Morita for your words and inspiration. To Terry Cannon (Baseball Reliquary) and Professor Richard Santillan (author of *Mexican American Baseball in the Central Coast*), thanks for introducing me to Jerry Roberts, Will Collicott and The History Press to allow our story, "pioneers" and legacy to have a rebirth. To the NBRP board, founding members and charter members, thanks for always stepping up when needed. I always use the term "synergy" or "syncronicity" when the right people, places and things line up for all the right reasons, so thanks to Jack Sakazaki, Steve Nakajo, Paul Osaki, Barry Rosenbush, Rosalyn Tonai, Gary Mukai, Chip Taylor, Junko Nakagawa, Sidney Mukai, Jim Noonan, Miriam Baum, Larry Gittens, Chris Terrence, Bill Staples, Kakei and Midori Nakagawa, Rick Walker, Steve Fjeldsted, Kurtis Nakagawa, David Okazaki, Tom O'Doul, Terrence Smith, Dr. Marshal Flam, Larry Rodgers, Maria Elena Cellino and Kevin Tsujihara for all being part of this magnificent synergy. Finally, thanks to my family—and especially my inner circle clan. Thanks to my wife of forty-one glorious years, Jeri, for allowing me to follow my passions and dreams; to Kale and Jenna for keeping our "samurai" chain stronger than ever and doing us proud everyday with your "beingness" and humanity; and to Katie and Olivia Rose for bringing us a Gosei (fifth) generation of extreme pride and a superlative future. Of course, I can't leave out the blessed "ones who went before us" because your spirit brings us all the success that we experience with our projects, goals, ideas and dreams of passion. *Namu Ami Dabutsu*, and as always, Health, Spirit and Aloha.

PREFACE

I have a mental image of Hideo Nomo. He's poised, motionless on the mound. His arms are extended high over his head, and he's holding the baseball in both hands. Slowly, he turns his back to the hitter, and then he recoils, firing a high fastball for strike three. I maintain that image along with the others of Willie Mays losing his cap as he rounds first base, stretching a single into a double; Hank Greenberg pounding a prodigious home run; Juan Marichal kicking his left leg high above his head in his windup; and Joe DiMaggio kicking the ground in disgust after being robbed of a World Series home run.

What all of these images have in common is that, while the players might have different facial features and skin color, they all represent the hundreds of immigrants and children of immigrants from around the world—including Asians, African Americans, Jewish Americans, Latinos and Italian Americans—who excel in America's great common denominator: baseball. What is so special about my image of Nomo is that he is representative of the newest group of immigrants to have a significant impact on major-league baseball—the players from Japan and Asia.

There is nothing new about the passion of the Japanese people—or of Japanese Americans, for that matter—for the great American pastime. In this book, Kerry Yo Nakagawa chronicles the one-hundred-year history of the Japanese fascination with the game, how it was exported to Japan shortly after the original rules of the game were codified, how the game grew in this country during the 1920s and 1930s and how the game was nurtured in Japan by many of the legends of the American game, including Lefty O'Doul, Babe Ruth and Lou Gehrig.

As with black players of that time, the opportunity for the Nisei to compete was limited to the formation of the Japanese American Leagues throughout the western United States and Hawaii, and they played against college teams, Negro League teams and teams of barnstorming professional players like Ruth and Gehrig.

With great sensitivity and perception, Nakagawa describes how, during World War II, Japanese Americans became the only group of U.S. citizens in history to be imprisoned as a group solely because of their race. I can recall from my youth how, during these extremely difficult times for our people, these American internees would organize themselves into leagues and even travel from state to state to compete on the baseball diamond.

Japanese American Baseball in California: A History is far more what its title suggests. It is a compassionate description of the immigrant experience of the Japanese people seen through the prism of America's grand game of baseball.

Noriyuki "Pat" Morita

FOREWORD

Growing up in Fresno, California, I was aware at an early age that baseball was an important part of our city's legacy. Our region has long been a great mix of cultures, and baseball was a common denominator. In the Central Valley California sunshine, we all began to thrive. By the 1930s, African Americans were playing in the Compress Leagues. The Nisei All-Stars were competing locally and even traveling to Japan on early barnstorming tours. In 1914, the prewar Twilight League from our area produced many professional players and major leaguers such as Frank Chance, who is in the Hall of Fame, and no-hit pitchers Monte Pearson and Jim Maloney, to name just a few.

Many of the local legends of the time were Japanese American baseball players. Known as Nisei, or second generation, these men and women loved their new country and loved playing what became known as the American pastime. Because of these Nisei pioneers, I realized that baseball was a part of the strong fabric of the Japanese American way of life in the San Joaquin Valley. It is a reflection of their positive immigrant experience of America and an American baseball story we all should know.

Japanese American baseball in California is that story. In this lovingly researched, beautifully produced book, you can see the teams as well as individual players and read their stories. Written by Kerry Yo Nakagawa of the Nisei Baseball Research Project, this book shows how the early Japanese pioneers made baseball a part of their lives and helped increase its popularity with other groups of Americans. It shows the rise to professional status for many among the Nisei generation in the 1930s and 1940s, despite the many prejudices they had to overcome. In compelling fashion, the book tells how baseball became a way to make life bearable behind the barbed-wire fences of the internment camps into which all Japanese Americans were forced during World War II. It tells how this rich cultural history continues today with Japanese American players, coaches, ballpark designers and plenty of Little League players dreaming of the majors.

Throughout the last one hundred years, baseball has been a sport through which Japanese immigrants and their descendants could put into practice both their growing American patriotism and their pride in their rich cultural heritage. In many ways, it is every American's story.

Tom Seaver

INTRODUCTION

Japanese Americans have been playing baseball for one hundred years. As fanatic about the grand old game as any other Americans—perhaps more so than most—they played the game around pineapple and sugarcane plantations in Hawaii, near grapevines and vineyards in California, deep in the forests of the Northwest and out near the cornfields of middle America. Their passion spread through the inner cities and found expression on church playgrounds, on neighborhood sandlots and in city parks.

For half a century, they played largely on teams and in semipro leagues of their own, for American society was not yet ready to welcome them. To the north were the Vancouver Asahi and to the south the Tijuana Nippon. In the east were the Nebraska Nisei and to the west the Hawaiian Asahi. All-star teams crossed the Pacific, journeying to Japan, Korea and Manchuria to compete with university squads and merchant teams. In the Roaring Twenties and the Depression-wracked 1930s, great Japanese American teams were competing at almost every level. They played Pacific Coast League clubs and all-stars from the Negro Leagues. They shared fields with Lou Gehrig, Babe Ruth, Satchel Paige, Jackie Robinson, Tony Lazzeri, Lefty O'Doul, Joe DiMaggio and many other stars.

Then came World War II, and hope and optimism were replaced with undeserved shame, humiliation and disgrace. Merely because of their race, Japanese Americans—alone among ethnic groups—were summarily relocated to detention camps in desert areas. Stripped of nearly all their possessions and treated as enemies-in-waiting by their adopted homeland, they mustered their dignity and determination—and played ball. Amid sagebrush and barren mountains, they cleared land for diamonds and built grandstands—and played ball.

After the war, Japanese Americans started over again, often in unfamiliar surroundings. They rebuilt their lives from scratch, assimilated into the mainstream as never before—and played ball. In reconstituted leagues, in colleges and universities, on integrated semipro teams, in Japan's professional leagues and, at long last, in the minor and major leagues of organized baseball, they followed in the footsteps of their parents and grandparents—and played ball.

In an often-quoted statement, Jacques Barzun wrote, "Whoever wants to know the heart and mind of America had better learn baseball." He might have written "the heart and mind of Japanese Americans." Baseball has been integral to the Japanese American experience. It provided more than a pastime, a way of escaping for a few hours on a Sunday afternoon from hard labor in the fields and cities. It helped to build community; it helped to nurture pride. It gave Japanese Americans something in common with neighbors who often wanted little to do with them. It gave them a way of becoming "American." But baseball also struck deep roots among Japanese Americans, just as it did among native Japanese from the time it was first introduced into Japan in the nineteenth century. And time and again, baseball has been a bridge between these two great nations, Japan and the United States, a connection shared by two very diverse peoples. After World War II, when American soldiers occupied Japan, it was baseball that provided the means of healing the wounds of war.

This book tells the story of the Japanese American odyssey as seen through a diamond and primarily focusing on California. The story of Japanese American players, coaches, teams and leagues has very nearly been a lost chapter in American and baseball history. Only today is it being rediscovered, to the benefit of America, baseball and Japanese Americans alike. A principal reason for this rediscovery is the traveling exhibition "Diamonds in the Rough," which tells the story of Japanese Americans in baseball through words, images and memorabilia. The exhibition opened in Fresno, California, in 1996 and has since been viewed in cities and towns across the nation, as well as at the National Baseball Hall of Fame and Museum in Cooperstown and the Japanese Baseball Hall of Fame in Tokyo. Also in the 1990s, a number of major-league teams, as well as the Hall of Fame, have given belated recognition to surviving Japanese American players of pre–World War II days. Now in their eighties and nineties, these venerable heroes once again stand in the limelight and hear the cheers of baseball fans. Their story, and the story of their ancestors and descendants, is a tale of a great journey, full of hard-won victories, devastating setbacks and new triumphs. The travelers on this journey are known by names designating the generations of Japanese immigrants and their descendants:

Issei—first-generation Japanese immigrants
Nisei—second-generation Japanese Americans
Sansei—third-generation Japanese Americans
Yonsei—fourth-generation Japanese Americans
Nikkei—Japanese Americans of all generations

So much of their story is wrapped up in baseball. If we were to dissect a Nikkei baseball, we would find that the center epitomizes the core members of the Issei and Nisei generations, the pioneers who created a culture. The fiber and strings would represent the communities, weaving their identities, loyalties and cultural affinities around their teams and players. The leather cover would symbolize the physical and mental toughness developed by the Issei and Nisei who endured the travails of settlement in a new land and the eviction and internment of World War II. The stitching bonds the Issei, Nisei, Sansei and Yonsei together and seals these family spirits for future generations.

Today, this symbolic baseball is being passed on to new generations. It carries with it the history, wisdom and pride of their ancestors. May they cherish this unique memento and embellish it with their own skills, discipline, courage, determination and sportsmanship, both on and off the baseball diamond. May they carry on the one-hundred-year legacy of Japanese Americans—working hard, keeping faith and playing ball.

Chapter 1

THE BEGINNINGS: JAPANESE AMERICAN BASEBALL IN HAWAII

In 1899 I formed a baseball team, made up of mostly boys in my home, and called it "Excelsior." Being the only team among the Japanese, its competitors were Hawaiians, Portuguese and Chinese. The team turned out to be a strong one and won several championship cups and pennants at Boy's Field on Vineyard Street in the Palama Settlement.
—Reverend Takie Okumura

The story of Japanese American baseball is nearly as old as the story of baseball itself. It begins in the Pacific paradise once known as the Sandwich Islands, where Japanese workers came to labor in the sugarcane fields. Some of these workers returned to Japan; many stayed. In time, a number of their sons, like so many immigrants of other nationalities, became part of the community by adopting America's national game.

MIGRATION TO THE MAINLAND

In May 1935, the first Hawaiian statehood bill was introduced into the U.S. House of Representatives. In October, six members of a congressional committee arrived in Hawaii to conduct statehood hearings, and 90 out of 105 witnesses testified in favor of statehood. In October 1937, another

Organized by Reverend Takie Okumura (behind equipment), the Excelsiors baseball team formed in 1899 in Honolulu and was the first Japanese American baseball squad. *Courtesy Makiki Christian Church.*

The Excelsiors practicing in Palama Settlement, Honolulu, circa 1900. There were forty-five boys in Takie Okumura's boys' home, enough to organize five teams. *Courtesy Makiki Christian Church.*

committee appointed by Congress held extensive hearings on Hawaii; 41 of the 67 witnesses favored statehood. Throughout these congressional hearings of the 1930s, the fear of a Japanese electoral majority was most often cited as a reason not to grant statehood to Hawaii.

It wasn't until August 21, 1959, that Hawaii officially became a state. Long before statehood, many gifted players yearning to prove that they could compete outside the pro ranks of the islands began venturing to the mainland and Japan. A number of players were sponsored by fellow Nisei working the farm belts of California. Some of these ballplayers opened the doors of opportunity at the turn of the century by speaking English and having the knowledge to read. They established farming leases and could cut through the red tape of Alien Land Laws and anti-immigration standards. By using the name of the American-born son (Nisei), Issei immigrants could purchase and lease the land. For new immigrants of any descent other than Japanese, life did not offer as many obstacles and gauntlets. Major-league aspirations were at the very bottom of the priority list because of the hardships of survival and discrimination.

Some of Hawaii's homegrown products did very well for themselves on California's baseball diamonds despite the void created by the absence of their parents and families. These early immigrants from Hawaii had friends or fellow ballplayers sponsor their trip over to the mainland to play ball. Their friends' families assured them work, food and lodging. On Sundays, they could feel at home again on the playing field. A spirit of familiarity and fellowship despite skin color and racial barriers brought out the best in these athletes. Italians, Germans, Jews, Armenians and Irish all were busy trying to establish themselves in America's new world. Baseball was about claiming a piece of space and proving how American you really were, if given a chance to play on a level playing field. It would be much more difficult for Japanese Americans to find the playing field in the "real" world.

Chapter 2

BASEBALL IN JAPAN: ORIGINS AND EARLY TOURS TO AND FROM JAPAN

We like to believe that countries having a common interest and a great sport would rather fight it out on the diamond than on the battlefield. We hope some day Japan can send to this country a team of players able to meet the best in the U.S. and prove to the Americans that the so-called yellow peril wears the same clothes, plays the same game, and entertains the same thoughts. In other words that we are "brothers." Once that conviction becomes universal, all of us, whether we live in Tokyo or Appaloosas, can sing together "Take Me Out to the Ball Game," and in doing so can forget the trivialities that from time to time threaten to disrupt our friendly relations.
—The Sporting News, 1934

B aseball tradition states that the game was invented in 1839 by Abner Doubleday in a small cow pasture in Cooperstown, New York. Thirty-three years later, the term "baseball" was first defined in an English–Japanese dictionary as *tama asobi* (ball playing). Later, an 1885 sports book defined baseball as *dakyu onigokko* (playing tag with a batted ball). These early references show how quickly the game took root in Japan. With its beautiful symmetries and mathematical logic and mysteries, the discipline of baseball found a congenial second home far from the country of its origin. It also became an important vehicle of cultural exchange across the Pacific. For American-born Japanese, baseball provided a connection to the ancestral country even as it enabled them to become "Americanized."

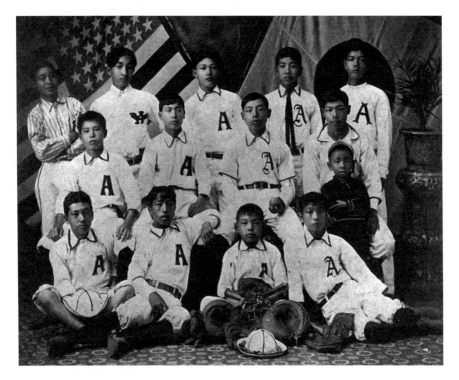

Founded by Steere Noda (middle row, third from left), this Honolulu Asahi team became one of the first Hawaiian Nisei teams to tour Japan in 1915, finishing the tour with an 8-6 record. *Courtesy Lilian Yajima.*

THE INTRODUCTION OF BASEBALL TO JAPAN

One of the first missionaries of baseball in Japan was Horace Wilson. This American schoolteacher brought the American pastime to Japan in 1872. Like most new resident teachers in this era, Wilson was considered a baseball enthusiast, and he had a keen interest in introducing the sport to his students.

Upon his arrival in Japan, Wilson became a teacher at Ichiban Chugaku (First Middle School of the First University Division) in Tokyo. The school, which eventually developed into Tokyo University, was renamed Kaisei Gakko the following year. That same year, a fairly large athletic field was built at the school, and baseball was soon being played with great passion and enthusiasm. Research by the Japanese Baseball Hall of Fame has indicated that baseball was

Considered to be a Japanese educator and baseball "missionary," American schoolteacher Horace Wilson introduced baseball to his Japanese students at Tokyo's Ichiban Chugaku in 1872. *Courtesy San Francisco Library.*

also introduced by American teachers in Kumamoto at the Kumamoto Yogakko (School of Western Learning). Other places where the game was introduced included the Kaitakushi Kari Gakku (Temporary School of Hokkaido Development) in Tokyo and foreign settlements in Yokohama and Kobe.

There was some opposition by the Japanese government to having baseball in the school systems. Many believed that baseball was a foreign entity and should not be played at Japanese institutions of higher learning. The proper Japanese student took judo or kendo (Japanese fencing) or disciplines that focused more on developing the mental, physical and spiritual aspects of the self. Horace Wilson, however, was a mathematics teacher who might have seen unique aspects of baseball that paralleled his teaching. In the game of baseball, you can be a success at the plate three out of ten times as a batter. You can be a legend if you hit four for ten. If you walk the first batter in an inning, seven out of ten times he will score; if you start the batter out with a strike, seven out of ten times it will lead to an out. One can speculate that Wilson saw that there were many statistical and mathematical truths that could be explored through baseball more than through any other sport or extracurricular subject.

Wilson could have seen the spiritual aspects of learning a game that requires a team of players to flow with one mind. He might have realized that his students could benefit from the many life lessons that baseball teaches. Pitchers were not always going to throw a no-hitter; batters were not able to hit home runs in every at-bat. Winning and losing were part of the fabric of the game. Even the physics of baseball presented mysteries that seemed mathematically unfathomable. The theory of hitting a round ball with a round bat squarely befuddled the minds of many who analyzed the sport. Horace introduced a new equation with geometric variables to the students, and they responded to his teaching. An early block-print image in a Japanese history book depicts a sketch of children playing baseball for students to research.

Another visionary pioneer in Japanese history was Japan's first baseball writer, poet Shiki Masaoka. Masaoka noted that baseball was a foreign game to almost all his countrymen. "There are very few persons in Japan who play baseball or understand it," he wrote. "Baseball had its start in America where it is a national game, just like sumo [wrestling] is to us and bullfighting is to the Spaniards."

Masaoka identified Hiroshi Hiraoka as a major "player, teacher and crusader for baseball." Hiraoka was one of the lucky youths the Japanese government had sent abroad to study Western ways. It was in New York City, where he had been ordered to go to school, that he encountered urban baseball. He got hooked on the sport and returned to Japan in 1876 and registered four "firsts" in Japanese baseball. In 1878, he organized the first baseball club and called it the Shimbashi Athletic Club (SAC). Hiroshi was an engineer for the Shimbashi Railway Station, the birthplace of railway in Japan. Near this station, he planned and built Japan's first field dedicated exclusively to baseball. The plot of land where the field was laid out belonged to the Tokugawas, the powerful clan that had ruled Japan for centuries. Hiraoka persuaded the family to agree to the sale of the land for the new Western game of baseball. The two other "firsts" credited to Hiraoka were the introduction of the uniform and of the curve ball. Hiroshi had brought back from his journey American baseball equipment, a uniform concept he copied and up-to-date knowledge of the game. He also became acquainted with Albert G. Spalding (founder of the Spalding Athletic Equipment Company). Spalding, then a pitcher for the Boston Red Stockings, gave Hiroshi several sets of baseball equipment and a new baseball book.

Because of Hiroshi's influence, the SAC took a lead role in spreading the word on baseball, with members coaching other teams in the Tokyo area. After the first baseball field was built, the first official game was with an outside team, Komaba No Gakko (Komaba Agricultural School). Two more teams were quickly organized: the Tameike Club (TC) and the Shirogane Club. These four teams dueled with one another for the right to challenge the Yokohama foreigner team. The outcome would decide the championship of Japan. Hiraoka and the SAC gave baseball a huge boost,

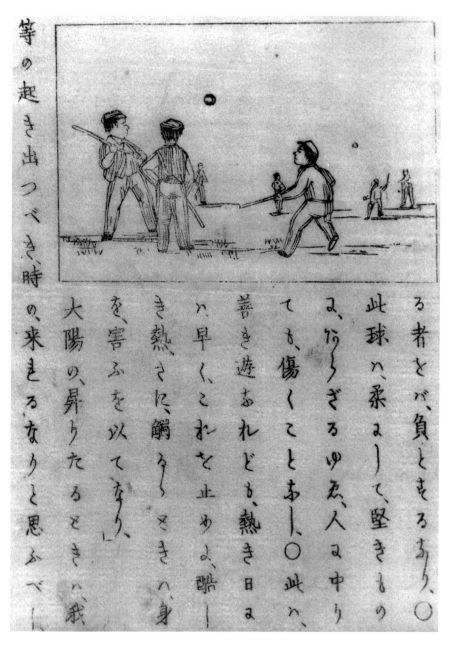

This 1874 woodblock print and simple description of baseball appeared in the Japanese history book *Shogaku Tokuhon* (Primary School Reader) and demonstrated the popularity that baseball had achieved in Japan only one generation after the game had been invented in America. *Courtesy Japan Hall of Fame.*

and schools such as Meiji Gakuin, Aoyama Gakuin and Keio Gijuku were quickly competing.

In 1886, a baseball team was formed at Ichiko (First High School). One year later, the SAC team broke up, with most of its players joining the TC. The most dominant schools of the future were the schools whose players were instructed by former members of the SAC.

During the 1890s, baseball in Japan was dominated by the Ichiko teams. On March 23, 1896, Ichiko won a historic and unexpected 29–4 victory against the Yokohama school at the Yokohama Country and Athletic Club. The game was widely reported in local newspapers, and the publicity spurred interest in baseball throughout Japan. Many alumni of Ichiko went on to coach at schools throughout the country.

In 1894, Kanoe Chuma, a former player for Ichiko, translated "baseball" as *yakyu* (literally "field ball") in the school's alumni magazine. Ever since, *yakyu* has been the established Japanese name for baseball.

EARLY NISEI TOURS FROM AMERICA

As early as 1914, there was a steady flow of teams traveling the "Bridge Across the Pacific," with teams from the United States going to Japan and Japanese university teams visiting America. This bridge of goodwill was very significant in terms of diplomacy and fellowship between the two countries.

Among the teams visiting Japan were those made up of Nisei. Since the semipro Nisei were competing throughout California, Oregon, Washington, Hawaii and the Rocky Mountain states, the next logical step was to travel to Japan. It was a golden opportunity to compete with college-level teams and heavily recruited merchant teams from Japan that took their baseball very seriously.

The first Nisei team to go to Japan was Frank Fukuda's Seattle Asahi. Fukuda was considered the father of Japanese American baseball in the Northwest. From 1914 to 1923, Japanese American baseball teams from Seattle visited Japan six times. The Asahi club was invited to Japan for the first time by two newspaper companies, Tokyo Nichinichi and its affiliate, Osaka Mainichi. It was common practice for newspapers in Japan to acquire more subscribers by promoting big sports events, and baseball teams from America were tremendous draws at the gate. In addition, the Japanese people were genuinely interested in the background of these Nisei who were born and raised in the United States.

Fukuda described the two major purposes of the Seattle Asahi tour: "One is to make our young players understand their mother country more deeply. And the other is to introduce Seattle to Japan and also study the current situation of Japanese commerce, which the president of the Seattle Chamber of Commerce strongly recommended." These goals would be shared by many of the Nisei teams that would follow from the States.

The Seattle Asahi's first reaction toward their mother country was one of curiosity. They seemed interested in everything—*kawarayane* (tile roofs), the small and bald hills and the *jinrikisha* (rickshaws). They were surprised at the narrow streets, the funny shape of *geta* (wooden clogs) and the poor structure of the Japanese hotels. Overall, their impression was not so favorable.

During their forty-two-day tour, the Asahi played twenty-five games against Japanese college and club teams, winning sixteen. A speech by Mr. Nakamura, an Asahi player, put the tour and the personal feelings of all Nisei into perspective:

Our club was organized in Seattle—such a nice and beautiful town—in 1909. The purpose of this club was to contact American people and understand each other through the various baseball activities. We think it is indispensable for us because there are still a lot of Japanese people who cannot understand English in spite of the fact that they live in an English-speaking country. That often causes various troubles between Japanese and Americans because of the simple misunderstandings. To solve this issue, it has become necessary that we, American-born Japanese who were educated in English, have to lead Japanese people in the right direction in the future. We have been working the last ten years according to this doctrine. All members here have really wanted to visit Japan. We have dreamed of meeting the people who have the same blood as ours. Now our dreams came true. It is almost impossible to express how delighted we are. One of the reasons for our tour is to observe Japanese society and economy, but the most important objective is to learn "Yamato damashi" [way of the samurai] in order to become a "Japanese" American-born Japanese, rather than to become an "Americanized" Japanese. And if we do something in American style with the Japanese way of thinking, we believe we can produce a superior combination of those two cultures. We have already observed many things that we had never seen or heard in the United States. From now on, we would like to continue to work hard to accomplish our goals under Mr. Fukuda's direction.

This speech encompassed the spirit of the many semipro Nisei teams that were to travel to Japan. Nisei ballplayers were making strenuous efforts to create a superior blend of Japanese and American cultures without losing their identity as Japanese. Fukuda popularized baseball among the Japanese people of the Pacific Northwest, but more importantly, he taught his youths the importance of dedication and both mental and physical discipline. He extracted many of the principles of baseball to enhance their lives after their playing days were over.

The Seattle Asahi's successful goodwill tour opened up the "Bridge Across the Pacific" for five other semipro Nisei powerhouses to cross over to Japan. The first were Steere Noda's Hawaiian Asahi, who landed in Japan in 1915. One of the island standouts who made the trip, Masayoshi "Andy" Yamashiro, would go on to play professionally in the Class D Eastern League in Gettysburg, Pennsylvania. Steere Noda was a champion of goodwill and sports fellowship, and he was so impressed with the tour that the Asahi would return to Japan in 1920 and 1940. The 1940 tour was called the East Asia Games, and on this trip, the Asahi competed with teams from Japan, Korea, and Manchuria, China.

The third mainland team to compete in Japan was the powerful 1924 Fresno Athletic Club. Chujun Tobita, manager of the Waseda University team, heaped praise on the Fresno players' baseball skills by saying they were "amazing" in their demonstration of technique and power. Kenichi Zenimura had formed the team by handpicking the best Nisei all-stars from the entire San Joaquin Valley. Before going to Japan, they had competed with semipros in the nationally recognized Twilight League in Fresno, Pacific Coast League squads and teams from the Negro Leagues. It was a great challenge for the university teams in Japan to see the difference in style of the Fresno club. Three years later, the team returned to Japan even stronger. Joining the team on its return visit were two Caucasian pitchers and one catcher who were well-established college-level players from Fresno State.

The San Jose Asahi crossed the Pacific in 1924, journeying to Japan and Manchuria, China, for their first and only barnstorming tour. Against the university squads, they were hammered pretty well, losing three out of the four games they played. But they regrouped in China, going undefeated in three straight games. Shigeo "Jiggs" Yamada, founder of the San Jose team, would recall, "I remember we were on the train, and as we got closer to the tunnel, all the Japanese passengers were busy shutting their windows. I just sat there, and as we went into the tunnel, all the black soot smoke from the coal-burning smokestack came into my window and

Left: Postcard picturing Frank Fukuda and teammate. *Courtesy Philip Block.*

Below: Homesick or a scouting report on opposing pitchers? These postcards were sent home by Frank Fukuda, one of the Seattle Asahi players, during the 1918 Japanese tour. *Courtesy Philip Block.*

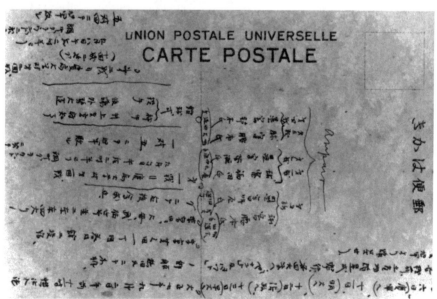

In 1925, cousins Tatsumi Zenimura, an all-star baseball and soccer player for Meiji University, and Kenichi Zenimura, a player for the Fresno Athletic Club, met in a game at Fireman's Park in Fresno, California. *Kenichi Zenimura collection.*

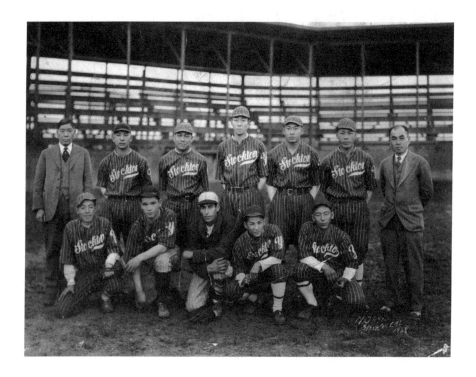

covered me. All my teammates got a good laugh." Jiggs was an all-star catcher and was famous for his cannon arm. "In one game, a player was taking a big lead towards third base, and the next pitch I threw down to second and threw him out. I liked throwing them out at second base that way," said Jiggs proudly.

In 1928, an all-Nisei baseball team from Stockton, California, stopped in Hawaii on its way to Japan. Coach Nobi Matsumoto led the Stockton Yamato Athletic Club. The team needed an extra pitcher for its tour and persuaded Henry Tadashi "Bozo" Wakabayashi to join. His decision to accompany the Yamato on the Japan tour changed the course of his life. He was so impressed with the country that as soon as he returned from the baseball trip, he decided in favor of college in Japan.

The Yamato barnstormed through Japan and Korea, compiling an 18-6 record against the Big Six universities and teams from major cities. Frank Mirikitani of the Yamato also had the distinction of touring with the Alameda Kono's All-Star Japanese Team to Japan, Korea and Manchuria. Other Yamato notables included pitcher Ty Ogawa and catcher Frank Ito. Harry "Tar" Shirachi of Salinas also pitched for the squad.

The Stockton Yamato Athletic Club (commonly called the Stockton Yamato) was organized in 1920 and existed into World War II. In 1941, it was among the top teams in northern California. The team's strength came in part from the coaches, who included Y. Ouye, a former pitcher for Keio University; Mike Matteoni, a shortstop for the semipro Sperry Flower Nine of Stockton; and Hugh McMurray, a former catcher for the Chicago White Sox. The Yamato played many professional and semipro baseball teams as well, including the St. Louis Cardinals, St. Louis Giants, San Francisco Seals and Sacramento Solons. They enjoyed many highlights in their career, including winning the Japanese State Baseball Championship in 1926 and playing in the National Invitational Semipro Baseball Tournament in Wichita, Kansas, in 1935.

Opposite, top: In 1924, the San Jose Asahi team barnstormed Japan, competing with the universities of Meiji, Waseda, Keio, Hosei, Rikkyo and Tokyo. These schools would later be known as the Big Six. *Courtesy Ken Iwagaki.*

Opposite, bottom: In 1928, the Stockton Yamato barnstormed Japan, compiling a record of 18-6. More importantly, the Stockton team introduced pitcher Bozo Wakabayashi (not pictured) to Hosei University, where he would later star. Wakabayashi would go on to play professional baseball in Japan in 1936 and become the first Nisei to be inducted into Japan's Baseball Hall of Fame. *Courtesy Jim Okino.*

In the early 1930s, Tom Tomiyama migrated to Los Angeles from Fresno and played with the famed L.A. Nippon. The Nippon were part of the Los Angeles County League and played other semipro merchant teams like the Tom Mix Wildcats, Paramount Studios, Knights of Columbus, Hollywood Athletic Club, San Clemente Dons, Pacific Steamship Company and teams from the Spanish American leagues. "I was a strong hitter and pitched pretty good too," the left-handed Tomiyama recalls. Also on the semipro integrated team were Andrew Harris McGalliard ("Bucky Harris"), Red Frasier and Gordon Ford. Ford, a middle infielder with the Nippon, remembered being introduced to the Nisei team through McGalliard. "Bucky loved playing with the Nisei guys, and we all played terrific together." In Japan, Andrew's real name was tough to pronounce, so the Japanese renamed him after Hall of Fame manager Bucky Harris.

George Matsuura was an all-star with the Wapato Nippon in Washington State and a pitching and hitting star with the L.A. Nippon. In 1931, the Nippon ventured to Japan, and George ended up staying and playing with the Nagoya team as a professional. The Nippon's tour was very successful, as they finished 20-5. George Matsuura and Andrew McGalliard of the L.A. Nippon turned to professional baseball in Japan. They signed with the Nagoya team in 1936. In 1937, catcher Andrew was chosen as the team's most outstanding player. That same year, Joe Suski would play for UCLA and the L.A. Nippon.

It was early on a foggy morning in 1937 when a group of California Nisei players boarded the *Chichibu Maru* in San Francisco. This all-star team of semipros from Northern and Central California was headed by Alameda capitalist Harry H. Kono and the "Dean of the Diamond," Kenichi Zenimura. Serving as an assistant coach was Kenso Nushida, former Mills College and Asahi star and recently a pitcher on the staff of the Sacramento Solons AAA team. The Alameda Kono All-Star team, managed and financed by Kono, was making its last tour to Japan; Korea; Manchuria, China; and Harbin, Russia. This goodwill tour would produce a record of 41-20, with one draw.

Four of the players stayed behind to play professional baseball: Kiyo Nogami and Frank Yamada, who were signed by the Hankyu Shokugeyo (professional) Nine, and Tut Iwahashi and Shiro Kawakami, who would play for the Dairen Gitsugyo team in Manchuria. Kiyo had been a shortstop at the University of California–Berkeley. He played pro ball and then, after a brief stay in college, became a multimillionaire manufacturing ice cream cones. Frank Yamada was a crowd favorite;

The 1931 Los Angeles Nippon team compiled a successful 20-5 record on its Japanese tour, and one of the Nippon players, Andrew Harris McGalliard (back row, far left), would later catch professionally in Japan with the Tokyo Eagles. *Courtesy Wally Matsuura.*

The 1937 Alameda Kono All-Stars, composed of Central and Northern California Nisei all-stars, compiled a 41-20-1 record on their Japanese tour, and four of the Kono players made a decision to remain and play professional baseball in Japan. *Courtesy Vickie Kawakami.*

For those who didn't get seasick, the dinner menu for a 1927 voyage of the *Shinyo Maru* offered smoked salmon, prime rib, boiled ox tongue and roast pheasant. For most of the ballplayers making the ocean crossing, miso soup and crackers were all their stomachs could handle. *Courtesy David Hendsch.*

posters of Yamada were visible in the Hankyu train stations throughout Japan. His famous nickname, *heso-den,* came from his style of catching the ball with his glove up at the waist near his *heso* (bellybutton)—a style ballplayers call the basket catch.

One of the all-stars on this tour was Shig Tokumoto, a pitcher from Hanford. Shig was an outstanding submarine-style pitcher. In one game in the 1930s against the San Francisco Seals, former major leaguer Walter Marty came up to bat. Shig recalled, "Walter hit the ball so hard that as it whizzed by my head, the first thing I did was turn around to see where the ball went—and it was already in the center fielder's glove." Shig vividly remembered the fifteen-day voyage to Japan with the Alameda all-stars:

When we boarded, we were below the deck. We were in the second class. There were rows and rows of cots or bed bunks, and the bell would ring and they would serve the food. Usually all I had was miso soup in the mess hall and water because once we got going, I was so sick that all I did was throw up. Dinners were Japanese dishes with fish, and on this fifteen-day tour, we had two days of practice and we would play catch up on the top deck. That's all you could do—just walk around the boat. It took me almost the whole tour to clear up my head from seasickness, but I had fifteen wins and even hit two home runs in one game.

Shig, Lou Tsunekawa from Stockton, Mauch Yamashita from Lodi and Cesar Uyesaka at the University of California–Santa Barbara are the only Nisei who have been honored by having a baseball field named after them.

THE LEGACY OF NISEI PLAYERS TO JAPAN

The barnstorming tours of American teams to Japan helped to popularize and strengthen Japanese baseball. From its origins in schools and sandlots in the late nineteenth century, baseball in Japan has grown to become a national passion as well as a major industry.

In the 1934 Major League Baseball All-Star Game, Hall of Famer Carl Hubbell of the New York Giants gained immortality by striking out fellow Hall of Famers Babe Ruth, Lou Gehrig, Jimmy Foxx, Al Simmons and Joe Cronin in order. That same year, Eiji Sawamura (left), an eighteen-year-old pitcher for the Tokyo Giants, struck out Ruth, Gehrig, Foxx and Charlie Gehringer consecutively. Sawamura's career ended tragically during World War II when a torpedo struck his ship off the coast of Taiwan. Sawamura is a member of the Japanese Baseball Hall of Fame. *Courtesy Kikuji Ryugo.*

Today, no one questions the wisdom of having two leagues in professional baseball to create competition and exciting playoffs. Japanese baseball adopted this system and created two leagues, the Central League and the Pacific League. Teams have often been named after their sponsors. For example, the pioneer club, the Tokyo Giants, are known today as the Yomiuri Giants, named for the newspaper that owns the team. Other proprietors have included companies like Hanshin Electric, Seibu Electric Railways, Hankyu Railways, Aichi Shimbum and the Lion Dentrifice Company. Contemporary professional teams in Japan are very similar to American sports franchises. Baseball is a billion-dollar business run by huge corporations. Most professional teams draft their players from the talent pools of high school and universities. (The Hiroshima Carp have a baseball academy in the Dominican Republic.) Teams are allowed to have four foreign players per team, regardless of skin color, race or origin. Just as in America, there has been some shifting of franchises over time. Today, there are six teams in each of the two major leagues:

Above: Catcher Tamotsu Uchibori and Hisanori Karita taking batting practice. *Courtesy Kikuji Ryugo.*

Left: In a 1935 contest, the Wapato Nippon led the Tokyo Giants throughout until the strong Giants team came back to win 6–5. The following year, the Tokyo Giants became Japan's first professional baseball team. *Courtesy Harry Honda.*

Central League

Yakult Swallows, Tokyo
Chunichi Dragons, Nagoya
Yomiuri Giants, Tokyo
Hanshin Tigers, Nishinomiya
Yokohama Base Stars, Yokohama
Hiroshima Toyo Carp, Hiroshima

Pacific League

Seibu Lions, Tokorozawa
Nippon Ham Fighters, Tokyo
Orix Blue Wave, Kobe
Kintetsu Buffaloes, Osaka
Chiba Lotte Marines, Chiba
Fukuoka Daiei Hawks, Fukuoka

While baseball is now authentically Japanese, Nisei pioneers are interlinked with the proud history and legacy of the sport not only in Japan but also in Europe, the Dominican Republic and many more countries around the globe. Many of the Nisei from Washington, Hawaii and California trailblazed on the fields and diamonds of Japan. Their vision and positive, aggressive American style of play helped to change and elevate professional baseball. Their insights and perspectives changed the ball fields into clinical laboratories of cultural and sociological study. The recent wave of world-class pitchers from Japan can be thankful that these "pros of the Pacific" opened the doors for them.

Baseball and the love of the game transcend borders, political ideology and cultural differences. Today, teams and players from Cuba, the Dominican Republic, Puerto Rico, Korea, Taiwan, China, Italy, Australia, Japan and the United States are internationalizing baseball competition. Professional baseball will someday become an international sport, and we will see a welcomed global celebration of a true World Series.

Chapter 3
DREAMS OF OPPORTUNITY:
ISSEI PIONEERS ON THE MAINLAND

Putting on a baseball uniform was like wearing the American flag.
—*Takeo Suo*

When the Issei, or first-generation Japanese immigrants, came to the United States, they had many positive expectations and dreams of opportunity, wealth and, for many, a new beginning in the "New World." They knew that acclimation to America would be difficult and challenging, as it was for most new immigrants, but they brought with them one constant as a badge to entry that aligned them with other immigrants: their passion for baseball. Baseball provided admission to the mainstream in America, even if it was only for a few hours on the ball fields. And Issei knew the game of baseball. It was the all-American pastime that they had already studied and adopted in the motherland of Japan.

Once they landed in their new country, the Issei set about establishing their livelihoods and townships, and very soon they began to develop a rapport with peers who played the game. One Issei, Takeo Suo, would say, "Putting on a baseball uniform was like wearing the American flag. But we wanted to show everyone how good we really were."

The Fuji Athletic Club was founded in 1903 by Chiura Obata (bottom, far right). The team included Setsuo Aratani (top row, third from left). Obata subsequently taught art at the University of California–Berkeley. His son Gyo, as a principal in the firm HOK Sport (Hellmuth, Obata and Kassabaum), would design and construct several of the most highly regarded baseball facilities in America, including The Ballpark at Camden Yards in Baltimore, Jacobs Field in Cleveland, Coors Field in Denver and Pacific Bell Park in San Francisco. *Setsuo Aratani collection.*

Edward Tokuzo Daishi (top row, center), grandfather of Lenn Sakata of the 1983 world champion Baltimore Orioles, was the manager of the Nippon plantation team. *Courtesy Marge Sakata.*

Struggling for Survival and Acceptance

Most of the early Japanese immigrants were young men who initially came as laborers with the intention of returning to Japan with the savings from their earnings in America. In the 1880s, industrialization and modernization of Japan deflated the yen so severely that in the rice industry alone, 300,000 Japanese farmers lost their land. Southwest Japan, including the areas around Kumamoto, Hiroshima and Yamaguchi, was especially hard hit. Rural families dispatched a son—usually not the firstborn, who was heir to the farm, but the second or third—to earn wages as laborers to pay off the family's debts. These young Issei were recruited to work the Hawaiian sugarcane fields or by Japanese labor agents to work on the railroads of the Pacific Northwest or in mines in Idaho and Colorado. The majority of them ultimately decided to make the United States their permanent home. Issei women came over to join them, and later the children arrived to be reunited with their families.

Many of these Issei journeyed to the United States between 1885 and 1924. The pipeline of immigration came through the Hawaiian Islands. Toshio Nakagawa recalls his dad talking about the migration to the mainland: "My dad worked in the boiler room at a sugarcane plantation. His dream was to come to the mainland and farm. His boss thought he was crazy for wanting to leave his steady job and friends. But I guess he was stubborn, and so his boss taught him how to read and speak English. After he left the Islands and moved to California, my dad helped a lot of other Issei get started in farming because he already knew the language and could communicate."

The opportunity to own land was nonexistent for Japanese Americans in Hawaii, so many saw moving to the mainland as a way to eventually acquire land that they could claim for themselves. The laws governing immigration and land ownership were stringent, but there were a few loopholes, including one that allowed the Issei to own the property if he filed the deed in the name of an American-born child.

Some of the Issei who ventured to the mainland were samurai from royal families; others were farmers, cane workers, cooks, potters, printers, tailors, woodworkers, sake brewers, hairdressers and laborers. These Issei worked long, laborious hours in the fields, in factories and shops, in forests and fishing villages and on railways up and down the West Coast and across the Rocky Mountains.

Issei women were a source of strength for their families. They not only bore the next generation but also took on any job that would help the family survive. They were cooks, merchants and laborers. They needed tremendous

The Asahi players, barnstorming at a train station in Aiea, weren't conceited; they were just convinced that they were the best team in Hawaii. *Kenichi Zenimura collection.*

patience and endurance to maintain the threshold of sacrifice they had to face day in and day out. Infants, out of necessity, went to work with their parents in the fields. There, they were carried on their mothers' backs as the women toiled or were turned loose around makeshift shelters built to ward off the sun and biting insects. As they grew older, children learned to play among themselves and take care of their younger brothers and sisters. "Stick ball" was popular among the pack of kids who waited patiently as their parents labored in the fields. A bamboo stick or a tree limb and a ball made from masking tape were all that was needed for hours of entertainment.

But once the childhood games ended, the road to acceptance would be much more difficult and harsh than any of the Issei could have imagined. By the 1920s, a xenophobic spirit permeated the air, and their physical appearance separated them from the general population.

Issei were denied many civil rights and were excluded from purchasing or leasing land through Alien Land Laws. Anti-immigration restrictions cut off any hope of reuniting with relatives by totally stopping any entry to the United States by Japanese. The National Origins Act of 1924 effectively barred the Issei from attaining citizenship, and anti-miscegenation laws in many states prohibited interracial relationships and marriages. It was very clear that a wave of anti-Japanese sentiment was spreading quickly in the United States. For the Issei, the quest for opportunity turned into a struggle for survival that would test their character and spirit.

The Beginning of Community-Based Baseball

These strong Issei networked with their peers to build communities and settlements for the many families starting out in this enormous country. Issei parents along with their children, the Nisei, built churches, both Buddhist and Christian, wherever they settled. They erected community halls for use as language schools and places for plays and movies. They lined streets with shops that sold miso and tofu, candy confections, rice and noodles, fresh fish and medicinal herbs, as well as repair shops for bicycles, watches and tools. They operated hotels, bathhouses, restaurants, bars, pool halls and gambling and dance clubs that were scattered among the offices of trading companies, physicians, midwives and newspapers. In every rural or urban region, usually on the west side of the tracks, these areas were designated Little Tokyo or Japan Town. These segregated townships cemented the community and enabled the Issei and Nisei to connect with a cultural center. Cultural events such as the Obon (a lantern festival for the departed) connected the families to the spirits of their ancestors and were a festive way to reconnect the elderly and younger generations. The rhythmic sounds of the taiko drums and the sight of the dancers and colorful lanterns provided a traditional source of identity and pride in the community. Food and game booths lined the cordoned-off streets and church grounds. Oshogatsu (New Year's Day celebration) was celebrated to bring in the new year with hopes for prosperity and long life, as well as to start off the year's first day with tasteful and healthy dishes.

Another very important component of the Issei's culture and heritage was the labor they dedicated to clearing the areas around their churches and halls to build baseball diamonds. Issei carpenters and workforces set to work without the aid of any power tools, and soon baseball fields began to sprout in almost every rural Japanese American settlement. In the beginning, just a backstop was needed, but as the fans' enthusiasm grew, so did the ballparks. Eventually, wooden grandstands, bleachers, dugouts and concession stands were erected. Urban environments were limited by the available space, so community ballparks were used by many diverse immigrant groups. For the Issei, this was a chance to finally reach outside the inner circle of their Nikkei (Japanese American) community and establish new ties to white society, developing a positive sense of fellowship and mutual respect while exploring the American style of play. They organized their teams and adopted familiar team names from Japan. So began a new era of Japanese American baseball on the mainland.

"These Issei built their own baseball grounds. They were remarkable in that they did all these things for the love of the game. They wanted to see their young people play," said Takeo "Babe" Utsumi, a Stockton Yamato ballplayer. "My father was one of those enthusiastic Issei," he went on. "Even on hot days, they'd be so proper, sitting out there watching the game in their suits and neckties."

Alice Hinaga Taketa, who became a star Nisei player in the Women's Night League, also remembered the Issei's passion for the game. "The Issei, they understood baseball," she recalled. "If it was baseball, [my father] would drop anything to see it. Baseball was 'it' for the Issei. That was their *tanoshimi* [extreme happiness], something they looked forward to." Taketa became a standout pitcher and hitter despite cultural barriers. "Nisei girls were supposed to be ladylike and not play sports, but [my father] let me play—he liked the game."

Noboru Kobayashi, who grew up in Chicago, was another Nisei who remembered his Issei father's fondness for baseball: "I remember once when he took the day off from work and we went to watch a team from Japan—a touring team from Waseda University—play the University of Chicago. My dad was always interested in baseball, and if he took a day off from work, then it must have been important."

ISSEI TEAMS ON THE MAINLAND

Chiura Obata, an artist, painter, designer and teacher, founded the first organized Issei baseball team in 1903. The team, called the Fuji Athletic Club, was based in San Francisco. Obata was born in Sendai, Japan, and began training in freehand painting under the tutorship of Moniwa Chikusen at the young age of eight. He was trained and educated at Kogyo Terasaki in the Shinyo school of painting and by Gaho Hashimoto of the Kano

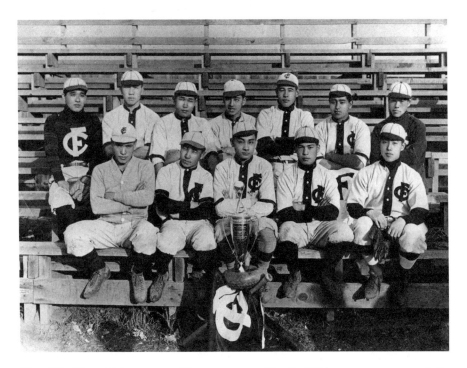

The Fuji Athletic Club championship team, pictured here in 1904, was among many ethnic minority teams to compete in inner-city tournaments in San Francisco's Golden Gate Park. *Setsuo Aratani collection.*

school, where he studied painting, sculpture, architecture, landscape design and handicrafts. In 1903, Obata arrived in San Francisco, where he accepted many commissions to decorate and paint murals in display rooms for various department stores and hotels. Later, in 1932, he would accept a teaching position in the art department at the University of California–Berkeley.

In between his art assignments and projects, Obata's passion was for baseball and his team, the Fuji Athletic Club (FAC). His design expertise and concepts were very evident in the team's logo. He incorporated "FAC" in a unique creative mass that requires close scrutiny to see all three letters. In the beginning, the uniform tops were laced on front; later, they evolved to traditional buttoned jerseys. Obata fancied himself in white shoes and chose to wear a beret rather than a baseball cap in the team photo.

The Fuji Athletic Club was the pioneering team that would represent the Issei ballplayers to larger segments of society in San Francisco. The city's most popular ballpark was Ewing Field, centrally located at Masonic

The name for Frank Tsuyuki's (bottom, fourth from left) 1904 KDC (Kanagawa Doshi Club) team was derived from their prefecture region in Japan and the word *doshi*, meaning "together." *Frank Tsuyuki collection.*

The Issei brought baseball with them wherever they settled. In the 1920s, George Sakamoto, a San Joaquin Valley farmer sponsored this team on his Cottonwood Ranch in California. *Tom Tomiyama collection.*

and Golden Gate Avenues. It was the hub of attraction for teams at every level. Merchant teams, religious ball clubs and Pacific Coast League pros all congregated at this expansive park. The FAC would enter this fraternity of American teams. Regardless of wins and losses, the team generated a presence in the baseball arena, where only the competitive forces mattered. Within the chalk lines, race, religion and stereotypes disappeared.

In 1904, another group of Issei players entered the scene. They called themselves the KDC. "K" stood for Kanagawa-ken, their native prefecture; "D" stood for *doshi*, "a bunch of guys" or "together"; and "C" indicated "Club." The KDC incorporated the uniform style that was popular in Japan. The squared-off caps with stripes were very common for the region of Kanagawa.

One of the core members of the KDC, Shohei "Frank" Tsuyuki, spent most of his life involved with baseball. Frank was born in 1882 in the Kanagawa prefecture. He immigrated at the turn of the century and joined the KDC baseball squad. Larry Tsuyuki would remember his dad telling him, "A lot of these white teams didn't take losing very well. As the game got closer to the end and we were winning, we would start gathering up our equipment, and as soon as the game ended, we would grab our gear and run." Frank was in the prime of his athletic career during these days. After the devastating San Francisco earthquake and fire of 1906, many local Issei migrated to other regions in search of work. Frank traveled south to Lodi and worked as a contractor on various ranches and farms.

Just as the Issei were gaining a foothold in their new country and starting to build a positive economic life, the Great Depression hit as markets around the country crashed. The Depression was a huge blow for the Issei, some of whom had spent almost thirty years struggling and saving to build a life with their families, only to watch their fortunes evaporate and work come to a halt. Frank Tsuyuki and his family eventually ended up in the town of Watsonville in Monterey County. His playing days were long over, but he still chose to stay in the game. Frank became a legendary umpire for the new Nisei leagues. Ted Tsuyuki, another of Frank's sons, remembers his dad umpiring: "He used to love umpiring these young Nisei games. The two strongest teams when we moved to Watsonville were both church teams. The Christian team was called the Aces, and the Buddhist team was the Kasei's. The Kasei's had this young pitcher named Tar who my dad really enjoyed watching." Harry "Tar" Shirachi would later achieve fame in a long career in Nisei baseball pitching for the semipro Salinas Taiyo.

Chiura Obata and Frank Tsuyuki were historically linked to the first recorded Issei teams, but baseball was becoming a cultural phenomenon in both rural and urban areas wherever Japanese immigrants settled. In Fowler, California, a newspaper reported on July 24, 1910, that "Harry A. Saisho, a Japanese enthusiast of Fowler, has just organized a Japanese team but is looking for a pitcher, catcher and third baseman."

Harry Honda's father was one of the founders of the Issei Wapato Nippon Baseball Club in Wapato, Washington. His dad immigrated in 1903, landed in Portland and traveled to Yakima Valley to work as a houseboy for a merchant's family in Yakima. He eventually opened a rooming house that was a popular and successful establishment for incoming Issei. Forced out of Yakima in 1925 when they were unable to renew the lease on their hotel, the Honda family took up farming in nearby Wapato. Harry recalled, "I suppose the Issei had some baseball when they were still in Japan, and when they came over here there were enough of them that they could start the Yakima Valley Japanese baseball club. And they played all around the Yakima area."

Across the Cascades in 1908, an Issei league in Seattle was organized, and two pioneering clubs—the Nippon and the Mikados—crossed over racial lines by competing with white amateur teams. A game between Seattle's Mikados and Tacoma's Columbias drew five hundred spectators in 1910. During this period, the father of Japanese American baseball of the Northwest, Frank Fukuda, a member of the Mikados, organized and coached a Seattle youth team. Called "Cherry," they went on to play against white youth teams.

Similar scenes were reenacted in other Japanese American settlements. In 1904, a young Issei named Kyutaro Abiko, a San Francisco newspaper publisher and businessman, started a utopian settlement known as the Yamato Colony in California. It was a community designed to welcome Issei immigrants and to stimulate organizations from within. Koko Kaji formed and managed the Livingston Peppers baseball team and received positive attention in the town's newspaper. These Issei pioneers were a paradoxical group who showed the way for the Nisei generation. They were fascinated with their adopted country, but they clung to the traditional ways of Japan. They were serious and extremely hardworking, yet they loved the leisure time of playing baseball and getting away with friends to sing, clap their hands and get rowdy. They were known as the "silent and model minority." But put them on the diamond as players or in the stands to watch their kids compete, and a new breed emerged. On the ball fields, they would cast off the moorings of the nonverbal and reserved Issei and unleash a volley of emotions—hollering, heckling, screaming and betting with the best of them. The Issei were voracious and passionate fans who experienced

In the early 1900s, mercantile industrialist Shinzaburo Ban's Issei team was the pride of the new immigrants located in the Portland, Oregon region. *Courtesy Homer Yasui.*

elation, suspense, disappointment, excitement, success and failure all in one afternoon. Sayo Kubo would say, "My mom and dad would say tomorrow is BBC [Baseball Crazy] Day, and I would be so excited." Sundays were usually reserved for this Baseball Crazy Day.

These Issei clung to the ideals expressed by American writer Francis Trevelyan Miller, who wrote, "Baseball is democracy in action: In it all men are 'free and equal,' regardless of race, nationality or creed. Every man and woman is given the rightful opportunity to rise to the top on his or her own merits...It is the fullest expression of freedom of speech, freedom of press, and freedom of assembly in our national life." Or as Chester A. Arthur, the twenty-first American president, said, "Good ballplayers make good citizens."

Putting on a uniform might have been, as Takeo Suo remarked, like wearing the American flag. But after donning that uniform and crossing the chalk lines, the Issei had to prove how well they could play. Fortunately, Issei were very good at the American game—and they felt good about being in America.

Beyond fostering a degree of assimilation, baseball was a leisurely game that offset the demands of intense physical work as well as the hardships and discrimination the Issei encountered. They were stadium builders, sponsors, coaches, umpires, gamblers, fans and, most importantly, dedicated parents.

Now this first generation was ready to pass the torch to the Nisei generation and set in motion the quest for acculturation and opportunities that came with their American citizenship. The Nisei's role was to assimilate the ideals and spirit of the West while maintaining the Japanese values that embodied harmony, perseverance and self-restraint. In this way, they would serve as a bridge between the two cultures as they cultivated the love for the game that their parents had instilled in them.

NISEI NICKNAMES

During the golden years of Nisei baseball, community spirit and civic pride in the town team were essential for the karma of the players. They took on their team names and wore their uniforms with pride. A baseball uniform was a badge of honor that gave them status in the communities. "I remember wearing my uniform all over town like it was my business suit. I felt like a diplomat for the team," said Mas Yano of the Delano squad. Many of the players also took on nicknames that stuck with them long after their playing days were over. Here are some of the nicknames, along with memories of how they originated.

- Herb "Moon" Kurima (Florin): "My old man used to make moonshine."
- William "Wild Bill" Kagawa (Lodi): "I threw real hard, but I was wild sometimes."
- Chi "T-Bone" Akizuki (San Jose): "I was pretty skinny."
- "Mutt" Furukawa (Hood River): "Let's just say he had a dog that looked like him."
- Yosh "Tubby" Tsukamoto (Florin): "I guess 'cause I was on the heavy side."
- Ray "Chop" Yasui (Hood River): "They knew my favorite food was Chinese."
- "Broken Arm" Kajiwara (Oregon): "He had a weird delivery, like his arm was broken."
- "Porky" Omori (Wapato): "He was a little thick around the edges."
- Harry "Jiggs" Yamada (San Jose): "They named me after the cartoon."
- Harry "Tar" Shirachi (Salinas): "They called me Tar after the tar baby in the Brer Rabbit story."

Eijiro Utsumi sells his confections to Stockton fans. *Courtesy Takeo Utsumi.*

- Takeo "Babe" Utsumi (Stockton): "My coach could not pronounce my name, so they said, 'Just call him Babe.'"
- Tsuneo "Cappy" Harada (Santa Maria): "I was always a captain of my sports teams."
- James "Step" Tomooka (Guadalupe): "…because of my foot speed, or lack of it."
- Kazuo "Pug" Mimura (Fresno): "I liked to get in fights."
- Tom "Dyna" Nakagawa (Fresno): "He hit like dynamite."
- "Porky" Takata (Watsonville Apple Giants): "He was on the porky side."
- Masao "Cow" Wada (Watsonville Apple Giants): "It was his heftiness, I guess."
- Sam "Lanky" Nagasi (Watsonville Apple Giants): "He was a long and lanky pitcher."

My parents used to have a soda fountain store called "Tsuruya," meaning crane and arrow. It was a popular stopover for the semipro baseball teams visiting Stockton to play our Yamato team. The 1935 Tokyo Giants even came to our place. My dad, Eijiro, was a baker and sold homemade anpan, manju, mochi and Japanese confections. He would take his goodies out to the stadium and sell them for the Stockton baseball club.
—Takeo "Babe" Utsumi

Chapter 4
BASEBALL CRAZY:
THE NISEI COME OF AGE

We would sure catch hell from the Nisei if we lost a game. If we won, we got a little praise, like, "yoku asobi mashita" [you played well]. *If you lost, they were so disappointed they wouldn't even talk to you. They'd give you the silent treatment.*
—*Yori Wada*

By 1915, a number of Japanese baseball teams had formed on the mainland. They were composed of young men who had learned the game in Japan and later immigrated to California. Prominent among them were teams in Los Angeles, Fresno, Florin, Stockton, Sacramento, Lodi and San Jose. There were other teams on a different level in Fowler, Hanford, Dinuba, Selma, Bakersfield, Salinas, Alameda, Walnut Grove, Isleton, Mount Eden, Oakland, Sebastopol and Monterey.

Beginning in the late 1910s, Nisei children started to make their marks

Above: Young Nisei children, in the early stages of what will become their lifelong passion, play baseball in a Stockton, California alley in the early 1920s. *Courtesy National Japanese American Historical Society.*

Opposite: In 1919, Alameda Nisei (second generation) children learned the fundamentals of batting at an early age. *Courtesy National Japanese American Historical Society.*

on the diamond. Nisei farmers on the mainland also organized their own baseball teams. These "farm teams" were among the first to feature Nisei players, many of whom were recruited from Hawaii to work the fields during the week and play baseball on weekends. The large influx of Hawaiian Nisei ballplayers was highly influential in developing baseball on the mainland to a more competitive level. These Nisei had developed their skills at an early age on the islands, where the ideal climate kept them playing year-round. As the Nisei came of age, the popularity of Japanese American baseball spread throughout California, Oregon and Washington; over the Rocky Mountain states of Utah, Colorado, Wyoming and Idaho; and even in Nebraska.

NISEI TEAMS AND LEAGUES

By 1920, eight teams played in a league that spanned the Rocky Mountain region, recalled San Jose resident Minol Ota, who played for the champion Wyoming Nisei team as well as an integrated semipro club. "Out on the prairie, we put up a diamond, backstop and dugout," he said. Ota's father, Chikahisa Ota, came to the United States in 1907 at the age of twenty. Most of the early Issei who settled in the Wyoming area worked for the railroad companies. Chikahisa Ota worked as a Union Pacific section foreman in Cheyenne for many years.

In time, Nisei teams ranged from as far south as the Tijuana Nippon to the Vancouver Asahi in the north and from the Hawaiian Braves in the west to the Nebraska Nisei in the east. Each young man truly played for the love of the game. Discipline, teamwork, loyalty, humility and dignity empowered them in victory and defeat. There was no financial windfall from playing on the semipro Nisei teams, but monetary gains were not the goal of these great ballplayers. They simply wanted to compete—and huge competitors they were. They played in city and county leagues, winning regional and state championships and dominating university teams. In many communities, Nisei baseball teams were organized by athletic clubs and church youth groups. These teams were formed with the intent of keeping the youth out of trouble by developing their character as well as their bodies. Baseball was seen as an ideal means of promoting Japanese values like respect, perseverance and teamwork while participating in America's national pastime.

Son of a section foreman on the railroad, Minol "Doc" Ota (front row center), was a Lovell, Wyoming semipro all-star in 1948 and one of the region's early pioneers and first veterinarians. Ota played with the Wyoming Nisei team as well as the all-white semipro Lovell team. *Courtesy Minol Ota.*

The all-Nisei teams were organized around 1917. In the early 1920s, Japanese American baseball on the mainland was brought to a new high with the introduction of young players from the Hawaiian Islands who were encouraged to play for the local teams. These Japanese Hawaiians raised the game to a higher level, enabling all-Nisei teams and their star players to merge into the highly competitive state and nationally recognized semipro leagues. In the 1920s, the Northern California Japanese Baseball League formed semipro teams like the Alameda Taiiku-Kai, the Lodi Templars, the Mount Eden Cardinals, the Oakland Merritts, the San Jose Asahi, the Sebastopol Sakuras, the Stockton Yamato and the Walnut Grove Deltans. The Deltans featured such players as Tom Yagi (who was also a Johns Hopkins University star), Flu Inaba, Harry Shironaka and George Watanabe. The Central Valley Independent League included the Clovis Commodores, the Fresno Athletic Club (FAC) the Guadalupe Packers (with the Tomooka and Iriyama brothers), the Sacramento Nippon (with June and Kay Miyagawa, two brothers who played baseball at Harvard), the Isleton

Above: In 1935, the San Jose Asahi defeated the powerful Tokyo Giants on a bases-loaded single up the middle by pitcher Russ Hinaga. *Courtesy Henry Honda.*

Left: Harry Shironaka (center) was a Walnut Grove all-star in the 1930s and at age eighty-eight was still captain of the Kids 'n Cubs softball team in Fort Lauderdale, Florida. *Courtesy Harry Shironaka.*

Purple Waves, the Salinas Taiyo, the San Luis Obispo Templars, the Arroyo Grande Growers (with Mr. Baseball himself, Kaz Ikeda, and his brother Sab), the Monterey Minatos (who featured five brothers of the Miyamoto clan) and the Watsonville Apple Giants. These and many more teams had fierce rivalries that continue to this day. They gave community to the little towns that grew up around the vegetable farms, citrus groves and packinghouses. They sent a clear message to the dominant white society that the Nisei would play this game despite exclusionary laws and despite hostility toward persons of Japanese ancestry. "It was about claiming a place in America where we all could be equal on a level playing field," says Harry Shirachi.

What an incredible range of names these Nisei had—from the Portland Midgets, Cortez Wildcats and San Pedro Skippers to the Salinas Taiyo and the Buddhist Bussei. Many of the teams' nicknames reflected the spirit of the players. The Portland Midgets, for example, were physically small Nisei players and eventually adopted the name after finding humor in it themselves. Many teams took on names that were Japanese in origin, such as Asahi (Rising Sun), Nippon (Japan), Sakura (Cherry Blossom), Taiyo (Sun) and Yamato (Japanese Spirit). Some team names went with the teams' church affiliation, such as the YMBA (Young Men's Buddhist Association). Others reflected the teams' location, such as the Wapato Nippon, Hood River Nisei, Cottonwood Issei, Walnut Grove Deltans, Guadalupe Packers, Oakland Merritts and Isleton Purple Waves. Sometimes the team name emphasized athleticism, like the Fresno Athletic Club and the Florin Athletic Club, while some teams were named after their manager or a sponsoring family like the Aratani Team, Maruko, Kono-All-Stars and SBAN (Shinzaburo Ban). Members of the L.A. Nippon often were called the Nips, a name that would seem racist if the players themselves had not been the ones to adopt this derivation. A number of the players even had "Nips" sewn on their uniforms.

White America was telling Japanese Americans that it was not possible for their families to immigrate to this country anymore and that it was not possible to purchase land or have interracial relationships. Japanese Americans were told that they could live only in certain rural areas or sections of cities and that the only contact whites would have with their culture was through stereotypical media portrayals and cartoons. But through baseball there was a universal language. Once players crossed the chalk lines, they could stage a battle for superiority and bragging rights, and they could show that they could compete at any level. Most importantly, they could display a love for the game that was the equal of any other American's. "In playing

The rabid enthusiasm of these fans helped to define the term "Baseball Crazy" (BBC) Day. *Courtesy Dawn Kawamoto.*

both skillfully and with genuine enjoyment, we were showing white America we shared their love of the game," George Tamura says. "Baseball was our way of communicating to white America our way of earning respect." At baseball games, new immigrants from different countries could sit side by side in the stands and take equal pride in watching their sons play a game they understood completely. Irving Raven, whose father was from Denmark, recalled, "My dad didn't speak a stitch of English, and his neighbor Hisataro didn't speak much either. But they would sit there and grin and eke out a few one-word adjectives during the game and have a great time. They developed a great bond."

Pete Mitsui, an original member of the San Fernando Aces, remembered the days when the team would pile into two old Model Ts and make the long, dusty thirty-mile drive to Oxnard or San Pedro for a Sunday double-header: "These were dinky, sleepy little towns, and about the only thing the hardworking people had to look forward to on their day off was a ball game. It was a social thing—free entertainment, a picnic, a get-together for neighbors from all around."

The Aces and other Nisei teams represented a subculture within American baseball that embraced many levels of play. There was the A-league, which represented semipro ability; the B-league, which was high school level; and the C-league, which was junior high level. But age was not the key factor; what mattered was only your ability to play the game.

THE BASEBALL SUTRA

The Baseball Diamond Sutra, by Helen Tworkov, tells a peculiar story about Abner Doubleday, the man traditionally credited with laying out the first baseball diamond in 1839 in Cooperstown, New York (today the home of the Baseball Hall of Fame and Museum). Doubleday was a member of the Theosophical Society and had a close friendship with the society's founder, Madame Blavatsky. He was also familiar with Buddhism, and some Buddhist baseball enthusiasts have claimed the "Father of Baseball" as one of their own for infusing his American game with mystical Buddhist numbers: nine innings, nine players, three strikes. Even the field has been taught as an esoteric reference to the Diamond Sutra, ancient Mahayana Buddhist scripture. According to modern historians of the sport, Doubleday's association with baseball is more mythic than actual—yet one great mystery remains. The number of stitches (sutra literally means "thread") on a baseball, 108, is the product of 9 times 3 times 4, the same number of Buddhist prayer beads on a sacred mala (wreath), as well as the number used ritually throughout Buddhist cultures. Even if history disproves Doubleday's influence on baseball, Buddhist sages tell us that there are no coincidences.

For the Nisei, baseball was often associated with churches. Many Issei had introduced the game to their peers in Sunday school as a fun and social sport that was genderless. Both boys and girls participated and competed, forming many church teams. The girls' team in Fresno was called Lumbini (after Buddha's Lumbini Garden). Throughout California's Central Valley, church teams competed against one another.

A close-knit community was essential for Japanese Americans in the 1920s and 1930s. The primal protection of numbers cemented their faith, relationships and family. Church and ballpark—not necessarily in that order—were strong symbols of their faith. The Nisei quietly expressed their love for God, Buddha, Jesus or whomever their faith worshiped under the church's roof. In the ballpark bleachers, they expressed themselves in ways that were not at all typical of the reserve usually associated with

The Fresno Athletic Club team captured the 1922 Japanese American championship. These semipros dominated California in the early 1920s. *Frank Kamiyama collection.*

Japanese Americans. On these hallowed grounds, the Nisei could feel the love of their parents cheering them on to victory. Where else could Issei and Nisei go to express their love and support for one another and vent their emotions? This is exactly why baseball became such a favorite pastime and played such a long and important role in Japanese American communities. Barred by racial prejudice from players in white leagues, Nisei organized and played among and against themselves. Jere Takahashi, a professor at the University of California–Berkeley, would say, "The importance of identity and community participation was very crucial to the survival of Japanese Americans prewar." Baseball, no less than the church and other community endeavors, helped to define and strengthen the Nisei generation.

THE GOLDEN AGE OF NISEI BASEBALL

The 1920s and 1930s were the golden age of Nisei baseball. Every community with enough players had a baseball team. Leagues flourished, and Nisei in Japanese American communities all over the West went baseball crazy. Fans of all ages packed the grandstands on Sunday afternoons, with crowds often numbering in the thousands for the big A-league games. No other social event could match the power of baseball in bringing people together. The Issei men, in particular, were fanatical in their support of Nisei baseball. Not only were the Issei the loudest and most numerous fans, but they also built the baseball fields, provided financial backing for equipment, sponsored most of the tournaments and even drove their sons to games in distant towns. The players never made any money in these Sunday contests aside from sometimes collecting for their expenses, but they always looked forward to the post-game victory ritual of relaxing in the *ofuro* (Japanese-style baths) and enjoying a meal at a local China Meshi (Chinese restaurant).

The Issei were now past the point of playing baseball, but they remained active in the game by umpiring, coaching, sponsoring, supporting and rooting. Gail Nomura observed, "Like most other immigrant groups in America, the first Japanese generation could share a common love for baseball with their second-generation American-born children."

George "Pop" Suzuki would say, "A good team will never have to worry about getting backing from their townsmen…Practically every member of the community who can walk finds his way to the local stadium to watch their pride and joy perform." Babe Utsumi of the Stockton Yamato recalled, "If we lost, it was nothing but *monku* [complaining]. *Yamato damashi ganai* [Your spirit was not in it]."

These Nisei were as American as baseball. Their baseball activities grew to new heights, reflecting a renewed optimism in finding a place in America. Naturally, top-notch teams developed in cities with large Japanese American populations, but many small towns boasting homegrown talent also fielded powerhouse A-team quality players and leagues. Much like the Negro Leagues for African Americans and the women's professional leagues, Nisei baseball provided a vital and vibrant way for Japanese Americans to participate in America's pastime.

Herb "Moon" Kurima, a pitcher for the Florin Athletic Club, recalled, "We couldn't join any league back then because the league competition began in June, and that was always time for our strawberry harvest. We had to finish our work before we could play ball." This time factor did not stop the Florin club from developing competitive rivalries with some of the top Nisei teams in Northern California, such as Walnut Grove, Sacramento, Marysville and Lodi. Although they played with passion and skill, most Nisei understood that pursuing a professional baseball career was a very risky decision. Rather than leave home to fight long odds, hostility, prejudice and discrimination, Nisei ballplayers chose to stay close to home, near family and friends, and play community baseball.

THE SAN FERNANDO ACES

The history of the Aces can be traced through such venerable former players as Barry, James and George Tamura; Pete Mitsui; and Ted Yoshiwara. The Tamura brothers' father sailed to the United States on a clipper ship in 1910 and settled down to farm a dusty patch of land in the San Fernando area. Among George's most vivid childhood memories are those of watching his brothers and Pete Mitsui play for the Aces before he finally was old enough to take over at shortstop. As youngsters, their parents enrolled them in Saturday classes to learn the Japanese language. During their lunch break, they would dash out to the baseball field for an hour or so before returning to class, usually late. "Our teacher would see us coming in all sweaty and say, 'You guys stink!'" James Tamura remembered.

Pete Mitsui was sixteen when the San Fernando Nippon formed in 1930, playing teams of white players from Reseda, Chatsworth, Van Nuys and Zelzah (now Northridge). In 1934, the team changed its name to the Aces and joined the Japanese Athletic Union. A few of the players owned Model-T or Model-A Fords, and when the Aces began playing other Japanese American teams, they would pile into the cars and make hour-long treks to Santa Barbara, Oxnard and San Pedro.

Pete Mitsui was the team's star pitcher as well as a good hitter, and he was an all-time Japanese Athletic Union all-star. Pete was the king of the Aces both on the mound and off the diamond. He also played on the L.A. Nippon team that barnstormed around the state, playing the best opponents they could find, often on other ethnic teams. With no major-league baseball west of St. Louis and baseball's color line still in effect, an occasional brush with a big-leaguer was a huge deal. Company-sponsored teams recruited Division I college players, Pacific Coast League players and also major leaguers back home for visits. "We had some great athletes in those days who weren't out to beat each other. I went up to bat against future Detroit Tiger George Vico. When George released a nasty forkball, it hit me right on the top of the head. This was long before they required players to wear helmets. All we

The pride of the San Fernando Valley, led by Pete Mitsui, the Aces of the 1930s toured throughout Southern California. *Courtesy Pete Mitsui.*

Future major leaguer George Vico (top row, third from left) stands head and shoulders over his Nisei teammates, including Pete Mitsui (top row, fifth from left), the 1939 San Fernando Valley Tire city champs. *Courtesy Pete Mitsui.*

had were our caps. I was pretty dazed for a while," said Mitsui. Red Barrett was another major leaguer who played with the Nisei. Five generations of Aces as Yonsei and Gosei's are still currently competing in Fresno, Florin, Lodi, San Francisco and Hawaii.

THE SAN PEDRO SKIPPERS

On a day in 1939, the fog still blanketed the ballpark as the fans filed in. Through the haze, they heard the rapid pop of balls smacking into mitts as the teams warmed up before the game. The foghorns in the background, the seagulls overhead and the smell of salt air reminded the fans that they were sitting in Skippers Field, home of the San Pedro Skippers, a powerhouse dynasty of the Japanese Athletic Union. The semipro Skippers were headquartered in the fishing village of Terminal Island.

This small island had a population of about three thousand Nikkei and recruited some of the best Nisei ballplayers in the metropolitan Los Angeles area. Most were homegrown wharf urchins who loved to play baseball. The Issei sponsors of Terminal Island had made sure that their children would have a first-class facility to accommodate the hundreds of fans who flocked to the games.

Kazuichi Hashimoto was the coach and director of the harbor squad. His son, Ichii Hashimoto, was an all–Southern Junior College all-star and third baseman for the Compton Tartars. In 1939, he hit .500 for the Skippers. Four other starters hit above the .400 mark that year, while the rest of the team had better than a .300 average. Besides Hashimoto, other college players on the team included Dick Kunishima of Whittier College and Frank Takeuchi of the University of Southern California. The Skippers tremendous speed and hitting ability were bolstered by the home run power of brothers Tee and Jimmy Okura. The pitching ace was Pee Wee Tsuda. "We averaged about fourteen runs a game during the glory years of the '30s," said home run hitter and, later, president of the Terminal Islanders, Yukio Tatsumi. "The Issei were big supporters of our team and league and were proud of hosting games at our Skippers Field. If it weren't for the war, this team would have stayed on top of the semipro heap for years to come in Southern California."

One of the more amazing upsets during the Skippers' prewar dynasty years was accomplished by the Lodi Templars. The game pitted the champions of the

The powerhouse of Los Angeles was the 1939 San Pedro Skippers, who averaged fourteen runs per game. Also known as the Terminal Islanders, the potent San Pedro lineup featured four hitters who batted over .300, four additional hitters who batted over .400 and Ichi Hashimoto (top row, fourth from left), who batted .500! *Courtesy Yukio Tatsumi.*

Japanese Athletic Union and the strong Northern California Japanese Baseball League. Coached brilliantly by Nobi Matsumoto, the Templars held the Skippers to single digits and won the Nisei state championship. Pitchers "Wild Bill" Kagawa, Oki Okazaki, Mas Okuhara, Shot Iwamura, Johnny Hiramoto, Sammie Ichiba, Matsuo Okazaki, Sam Funamura, Red Tanaka, Keizo Okuhara and Kazuto Ito all contributed to the classic championship battle. "This was one of the only times I can remember only getting one hit," said Yukio Tatsumi.

THE ALAMEDA TAIIKU-KAI (ATK)

Another baseball squad familiar with ocean air and ships sailing in the bay near its field was the famed Alameda Taiiku-Kai (ATK). From 1918 to 1940, the ATK earned a reputation as one of the elite Japanese American

The home run king of the Alameda Taiiku-Kai (ATK) team in the 1920s was Mike Nakano. Note the clipper ship on San Francisco Bay in the background. *Courtesy National Japanese American Historical Society.*

baseball teams in Northern California. Widely known for producing top-notch players and enthusiastic community supporters, the ATK contributed much to the annals of Japanese American sports history.

The roots of the ATK baseball team go back to 1913, when the team was founded by a group of Issei who brought their love of baseball from Japan. These players eventually formed the nucleus of the Alameda Young Men's Buddhist Association (YMBA) Baseball Club in 1916. By 1918, however, the team changed its name to ATK in order to be inclusive of both Buddhist and Christian Japanese Americans. Instrumental in the development of the ATK were Nisei manager Takurisu Morita and the legendary players who proudly wore the ATK uniforms: pitchers Ben Tanizawa and Sam Rokutani, along with other core members such as Sai Towata, Kiyo Nogami, Maz and Mike Nakano, Shizuto Kawamura, Tad Hayashi, Shug Madokoro, Taro Takeda and John Hanamura. In 1918, Sai Towata led his famous Otto Rittler–coached team to a Northern California high school championship. On this squad were future major leaguers Dick Bartell and Johnny Vergez. Sai was the shortstop and cleanup hitter for the team. After the season, Vergez and Bartell were signed to pro ball; the team's MVP, Towata, was never offered a contract.

The home field of the ATK, built by enterprising Issei and Nisei players on a vacant lot on the corner of Walnut and Coleman Avenues, was known as ATK Diamond. With a well-tended field and grandstands built from the ground up with very primitive materials, ATK Diamond was the setting for many Sunday afternoon games in the summer. Most of the ATK's games were played against rival Northern and Central California teams from San Jose, Stockton, Fresno and Sacramento. When the college teams from Japan came to play, however, the ATK were more than willing to give them a game. After home games, a ritual trip to the Morino Bath House was made for free baths, followed by ice cream at the Takata Candy Store and, finally, dinner in Oakland's Chinatown. Although ATK players were not paid, the team received monetary support through contributions from Nisei boosters and by passing the hat at games. On occasion, the team would show benefit movies at the local Buddhist temple to help subsidize the purchase of equipment and uniforms and to pay for hotels and meals during their out-of-town trips. Although he pitched for the prewar Oakland Merritts, Goro Suzuki would later become a famous community singer, dancer and actor. To avoid the concentration camp experience, he changed his name to Jack Soo and later was a celebrity on the hit television series *Barney Miller*.

THE FLORIN ATHLETIC CLUB

The Florin Athletic Club (Florin AC) was founded in 1914. It is recognized as one of the pioneer Japanese American baseball teams. By the 1920s and 1930s, the Florin Athletic Club had achieved notoriety as a perennial powerhouse within the fast A Division of the Northern California baseball circuit. Every Sunday in the summer, the Florin community came out to cheer on their home team.

The Florin team was unique in that it did not belong to an organized league during the prewar years. The 1937 and 1939 editions of the club are remembered as two of the strongest before World War II. Moon Kurima was the star pitcher and coach of the Florin Athletic Club for more than thirty years. Some of the other legendary players who came out of the club included Bill, Yosh and Jim Tsukamoto; Buddy Yasukawa; T. Yasui; Tom Fukushima; Sauda Yasui; and Roy Kawamura.

THE WATSONVILLE APPLE GIANTS

Although they won the Watsonville city championship in 1926, the Watsonville Apple Giants were remembered more for their nicknames. These Nisei played from 1924 to 1929. They were capable of beating any semipros in the area and formed the team to compete against locals in San Francisco, Monterey and Columbia Park, as well as the San Jose Asahi. Here is the way they used to stack up: "Porky" Takata, catcher; Harry "Tar" Shirachi, pitcher; Masao "Cow" Wada, first base; "Yonnie" Yamasaki, second base; Harry Ogi, shortstop; Benny Matsuda, third base; Joe Morimoto, left field; Sam "Lanky" Nagasi, centerfield and pitcher; and Tommy "Gun" Matsuda, right field. Most of the players were merchants during the week and, for five golden years, pros on Sunday.

Many players from this Watsonville, California all-star team fell one game short of facing the immortal Satchel Paige and his Bismarck, North Dakota team in the National Baseball Congress Tournament in 1935. *Courtesy Don Shirachi.*

THE NISEI ATHLETIC CLUB, HOOD RIVER, OREGON

In 1930, a group of young Nisei ballplayers in Hood River, Oregon, decided to form a team. Because there were so few Nisei men around the ages of seventeen to twenty from Hood River, the founders of the club reached out to places such as Bingen, White Salmon and Dallas Port on the Washington side of the Columbia River and to Mosier and Deschutes on the Oregon side. Although the men who joined the Nisei Athletic Club (NAC) of Hood River came from different geographical areas, they had a lot in common: ethnicity, dual cultures, morals learned from their parents, Japanese language capabilities and experiences of racial discrimination. Most of the competition they faced in the early days was provided by local white teams who were also pick-up teams at the semipro level. They included the Hood River American Legion, the White Salmon Eagles, the Odell Parkdale, the Lyle Townies, the Hood River Wyeth Monties Bar Flies and Maupin. The NAC would develop such stars as Ki Yokawa, Koichi Uyeno, Smiley Takasumi, Kasua and Watt Kanemasu, Fred and George Kinoshita, Sash Migaki, Tutch Takasumi, Satoshi Tsubota, Ray "Chop" Yasui, Coon Yoshinari and Oregon State star Kay Kiyokawa.

The Wapato Nippon

In advance of the Great Depression in the early 1930s, tension rose again in the Yakima Valley of Washington because of heightened fear of a new wave of Asian workers coming to the valley. The primary industry was lumber, and it was going through a severe slowdown. There was very little work, and an influx of Japanese added to the paranoia that Asian newcomers were taking work away from the locals. Urico Ito recalled his family's farmhouse being dynamited in the spring of 1933: "With loud crackling sounds, the house was shaking. I suddenly woke up. My husband jumped out of bed, threw on his robe and ran out. Beside myself with shock, I followed him. Just as I took a couple of steps out of the house, the second explosion took place. Pieces of wood were lying within two feet of my husband. It was dynamite that caused the explosion. Some of the garage and some of the Dodge three-quarter truck were completely blown up." That spring there were six incidents of dynamiting and arson directed at Yakima Valley Japanese. In the small farming town of Grandview, a 1924 public meeting of the Ku Klux Klan attracted forty thousand people. About one thousand white-robed, unmasked knights formed a huge crescent within which five hundred initiates took the obligations of the invisible on a field illuminated by the glare of three huge crosses studded with electric lights.

Frank Fukuda (second row, second from left), the father of Japanese American baseball in the Pacific Northwest, managed this Wapato Nippon team in Washington State during the early 1930s. *Courtesy Harry Honda.*

The Wapato Nisei baseball team was hopeful that it could break down stereotypes of Asians and overcome racial hatred. Harry Honda recalled an experience the Nippon had at Roslyn, Washington:

> *We played in places where they'd never seen a Nisei. They turned up out of curiosity. When we moved to the Yakima Valley league, there was a team there named Roslyn that was a coal mining town. A real tough place. The whole town came out to see this Japanese American team play, and we played a real good game. Later, they invited us back. They appreciated us—maybe because they'd never seen a Japanese before. I thought that was nice because in those days Japanese had a tough row to hoe, you know.*

Everywhere we went, somebody would make some remark about us. You know, though, through sports, you can get rid of a lot of discrimination. But sometimes the fields weren't always level.

Umpire favoritism was a potentially sensitive subject that the Nippon always wanted to avoid but many times had to face. Shigeru Osawa, who played in Seattle against white teams, remembered the problematic nature of baseball officiating within interethnic leagues: "On occasions when the white umpires favored white teams, the white audience became our fans and didn't hesitate to cheer us on." In the Yakima Valley, each town team supplied its own umpire, an arrangement that could give unique meaning to "home field advantage." Yet the Nippon's umpire, Harry Masato, was popular with the visiting white teams. As Harry Honda explained, "Opposing teams never quibbled about our umpire because if there ever was a close decision, Harry would give it to the other team." Riding the umpire was part of the entertainment in the Mount Adams League, but as Honda said, "You figure a close decision would go the other way, but we didn't care. We were just glad to be playing ball and to have an umpire. All of our teams liked our man best. He was fair and honest."

One memorable game symbolized the Nippon's sportsmanship and restraint in the face of constant adversity. The 1934 Wapato town championship game became a morality contest in which it was reported that the all-white town team unfairly recruited talent from outside its jurisdiction in order to gain the advantage over the Nippon. There were even reports that the Wapato team had sunk to the level of bribing the umpire. The chaos culminated in the ninth inning, when the Wapato pitcher broke his leg stealing a base. The town team refused to play on, thus forfeiting the game. The Nippon players refused to accept the forfeit and offered gate money for the injured pitcher, as well as a benefit game the following weekend. The *Wapato Independent* wrote of the white team's shameful behavior in this game while extolling the Nippon's clean sportsmanship. This account was especially significant because up to this time, the *Independent*, a father-and-son newspaper, had shown extreme hatred for Japanese Americans.

The compassion the Nippon showed toward the Wapato team in this game helped to dissipate the bitterness against Japanese and became a very positive healing force for the Wapato community. The Nippon's conduct changed the perspective of many white residents toward the Nisei Wapatos. Moreover, a winning team is very difficult to ignore. Its victories eventually weave their way into the local fabric, and the team becomes adopted as a civic symbol. Harry Honda noticed that after the famous game with the Wapato town team, "gradually, the Caucasian public turned out to our games since we were doing better than the town team. The Nippon were identified with the town of Wapato, with the occupation of farmers working the reservation land and with their Asian heritage. We had a lot of fun playing the town teams, and we got a lot of support from the whole community."

For Herb Iseri, playing against white teams was free of racial tension: "[It was] just like playing a regular team. There wasn't any tension on the field with white players. I don't know about the spectators, but to the players, it was just another game." Herb recalled an incident in which an opposing white player broke his leg sliding into the Nippon's catcher, Art Kikuchi. "The money we made on the game, we put it together, both teams, and gave it to the guy with the broken leg," Herb said. Herb knew that the Wapato Nippon were as good as any town team in the Yakima Valley or in the state of Washington, but the quality of the team wasn't due to a systematic training regimen. "It's amazing, you know. You follow a horse around in the fields all day plowing up the land, and you practice one day a week and then play next Sunday. That's all we had time for, and we did pretty well."

In 1935, the Tokyo Giants came to the Yakima Valley to take on the Nippon. The game occasioned a tremendous holiday in the Yakima Valley as practically every Japanese family in the state deserted their farms to see the brilliant Japanese professional team meet the Nisei stars. In a close battle in which the Wapato Nippon took a 5–1 lead, the Giants battled back and won 6–5.

The Wapato Nippon represent in microcosm the spirit of many of the Nisei and how the highly competitive Nisei leagues and teams made the air around baseball light and comfortable for people of diverse cultures. It was an atmosphere that Japanese Americans were drawn into, and in embracing the cultural norms of baseball, the Nisei generation also gave to the game their own ethnic and cultural dynamic. Thus, baseball as an ethnic phenomenon was mediated by an assortment of factors. The Nisei players promoted messages about assimilation within American norms as well as ideas about higher values of playing baseball. The Japanese American community in the Yakima Valley, bound by its isolation and by patterns of discrimination, rallied around its baseball team as a marker of ethnic pride as well as a demonstration of achievement in the American pastime. In Nisei baseball, ethnicity was embraced and at the same moment subordinated as Japanese mapped their passage through and into American society.

JIMMY HORIO

One of the strongest Nisei to come out of the Hawaiian Islands was Jimmy Horio. After coming to the mainland, Horio joined the Los Angeles Nippon, one of the powerhouse Nisei semipro teams. He played four years for the Nippon, from 1930 to 1934. During the 1934 season, he moved to Sioux Falls, South Dakota, and played 140 games in the Nebraska State Leagues. He was hailed by scouts as one of the flashiest, smoothest players in the league. The Nebraska State Leagues were run by St. Louis Cardinals scout Charles Barret, who encouraged Horio to keep up his wonderful work. After completing a successful season in the Nebraska State Leagues, Horio went to Japan. He was immediately asked to join the Tokyo Giants, the first organized professional baseball club in Japan. As a member of the All-Japan team, he played against the invading major-league all-stars in 1934, including Babe Ruth, Lou Gehrig, Jimmy Foxx and Charlie Gehringer.

Horio's impressive work in both fielding and batting enabled him to make the Tokyo Giants squad that came to the United States. Many Pacific Coast League owners wanted to sign Horio, but Earl McNeely, the owner-manager of the Sacramento Solons, made the best deal for him. After the Tokyo Giants left for Japan, Horio became a

Jimmy Horio. *Jimmy Horio collection.*

full-fledged Solon player. He was the second Japanese American to don a Solon uniform, the first having been Kenso Nushida. When interviewed by a writer, Horio said that baseball "is the most important sport in Japan at the present time." Baseball in the United States is run on such a competitive scale that it gives a player a chance to graduate from a lower league to a higher one depending on one's work. In Japan, the professional baseball player league has not been organized yet, although the Tokyo Giants intend to start a league in the near future in order to give the Japanese fans a real impression of professional baseball like it is played here in America.

Chapter 5
BREAKING BARRIERS

*I always thought that Nisei meant "great baseball player" in Japanese. All the
ones I knew certainly fit that description.*
—Ken Wallenberg, scout for the New York Yankees

Although many Nisei players had the ability to play at the major-league
level, the raw state of xenophobia smothered any ambition to break
through racial barriers. In the early part of this century, racism permeated
virtually all aspects of life, and the Nisei hopefuls felt its oppressive
influence. There were other pressures on young players as well. Their Issei
parents were struggling to create new lives in the "land of opportunity,"
and they needed the whole family's support. With their focused work
ethic, a career on the fields meant agriculture, not baseball, to the Issei
immigrants. Starting off the day with a hook didn't mean throwing a curve
ball; it meant rigging up your line for the family's fishing boat. Gaining
a foothold in an adopted nation required constant physical, mental and
spiritual labor. Even if baseball careers had been a possibility, few Nisei
would have been able to take up the sport beyond recreation because of
the demands of daily life.

Despite racial barriers, ambition can lead a young player in a new direction,
and talent can sometimes transcend prejudice and level the playing field.
Nisei ballplayers had a strong competitive spirit—enough to vie with major
leaguers. A dedicated few made baseball their way of life and, through their
efforts, skill and ambition, paved the way for future generations.

The Setsuo Aratani (second row, third from left) company team of 1927 was a multicultural team of Latinos, Caucasians and Nisei who competed with merchant teams throughout Japan. The ten-year-old batboy (center) was Setsuo's son George, who became a Nisei baseball legend as well. *Setsuo Aratani collection.*

Since the beginning of the sport, baseball scouts and owners have used a tried-and-true set of criteria for choosing players. There are five essential abilities for achieving a professional ranking: to catch the ball under virtually any circumstance; to throw it with strength and precision; to hit the ball hard enough and frequently enough to achieve a good batting average; to hit it with power; and to run the bases with speed. Players who can perform these tasks at a world-class level should be accepted and respected anywhere. Because prejudice stood in their way, Nisei ballplayers tried to distinguish themselves with ability. Often they excelled in skill when compared with their professional peers. Still, for most of them, skill was not enough.

This chapter tells the stories of some of the teams and individuals who strove to break barriers and champion their communities through skill, courage and the will to elevate themselves above the norm. These Japanese Americans refused to lose and demanded nothing less than perfection from themselves and their peers. They were determined to take advantage of every opportunity their new homeland offered to those with the desire and ability to excel. Along the way, they had memorable encounters with a number of other Americans who also crossed the lines of racial segregation.

Aratani Team

Setsuo Aratani was a pioneering immigrant from Hiroshima who arrived in America at the turn of the century. His journey took him to San Francisco, where a group of men led by Chiura Obata were forming the first Issei team, the Fuji Athletic Club. Soon they were joined by another Issei team, the KDC team. These teams, along with school teams, merchant squads, pick-up groups and organized church teams, competed on diamonds like the city's Ewing Field and in Golden Gate Park. The sound of the festive fans cheering on the local teams was an addicting tonic for players and spectators alike.

These days of glory came to an abrupt end with the thunderous earthquake and devasting fire that leveled much of San Francisco in 1906. Many of the new immigrants were compelled to settle in other regions. Aratani relocated south to Guadalupe, California, fifty miles north of Santa Barbara. This coastal area had rolling hills, magnificent open land and lovely vistas, but more importantly to an earth-minded agriculturalist, it had deep, rich soil and an excellent climate. Aratani staked his claim and began to farm vegetables. He amassed acre upon acre of the prized territory, finally becoming the "lettuce king" of Guadalupe. His work ethic and pioneering efforts helped him develop over five thousand acres of lettuce and vegetable cash crops. It would require constant care and a huge workforce to keep this empire running smoothly.

Aratani never relinquished the passion for baseball that he developed in San Francisco as a member of the first Japanese Americans mainland team. The spirit of the Fuji Athletic Club prompted him to begin searching for the best athletes within the circle of his company employees regardless of ethnic background. Two of his workers, Fred Tsuda and Moriso Matsuno, had been teammates at Whitman College in Washington State. Matsuno was a strong pitcher, while Tsuda was an infielder. Their playing ability and college level of baseball knowledge prompted Aratani to have the two men interview potential employees who could also compete as good players for

Nisei slugger and baseball ambassador George Aratani played at Keio University. Compared defensively to Phil Rizzuto, George competed against the great Ted Williams and was coached by Hall of Famers Honus Wagner and Paul and Lloyd Waner of the Pittsburgh Pirates organization. *Courtesy George and Sakaye Aratani.*

the company team. He had a diverse mixture of Latinos and Anglos in his employ who took their work ethic to the playing fields. They worked hard but played harder. Assembling a salad bowl of players from different cultures, Aratani sponsored his Aratani baseball team. Lefty Nishijima, a ballplayer from San Luis Obispo, recalled Aratani's generosity toward players: "I remember Mr. Aratani would have these huge barbecues for all the players and family. He really made it fun for us." Most managers would have been content playing the local commercial teams in Santa Maria, Arroyo Grande, and San Luis Obispo, as well as the coastal regional teams in their area—but not Aratani. His Guadalupe Packers team even competed with the Central Valley "A" team, the Fresno Athletic Club.

In 1927, Aratani decided that his team needed international competition, so he sponsored a goodwill tour to Japan. The team boarded the *Korea Maru* for the fifteen-day voyage across the Pacific to spread the Guadalupe Packers way of baseball in Japan. Aratani took his ten-year-old son, George, and suited him up as the team's batboy. (Seven years later, George would help his Santa Maria High School team win the state championship.) After a scenic tour of the region around Tokyo, the team headed to Hiroshima to visit Aratani's friend Ikeda, who had made his fortune in sho-yu sauce (soy sauce) in the Hiroshima area before big conglomerates drove the small companies out of business. Informed that most of the team were used to showers and might resist the *ofuru* style of Japanese bathtubs, Ikeda installed showers in the team's custom-built quarters. He and Aratani then arranged for the team to tour the cities of Matsushima and Sendai, providing a rich cultural experience.

After the sightseeing expedition, it was time to get down to baseball business. The Aratani team traveled to Osaka, where it would compete against the strong Jitsugyo Yakyu-dan team, the company team of the *Osaka Mainichi* newspaper. Moriso Matsuno coached the Aratani team, and he relied on the leadership of players such as Walker and both Montez brothers. The team played at least four or five games, splitting the wins and losses. Young George Aratani was even allowed to pinch-hit. "It wasn't even close. I was ten years old facing a pitcher that was a man, but I'm glad my dad gave me a chance to bat," said George.

The fellowship and goodwill generated by the Aratani integrated baseball club in Japan was a huge victory for both countries. Years later, in Guadalupe, Keio University would challenge the Aratanis. The aging team of veterans also played the famed Tokyo Giants. "I remember the Russian pitcher Victor Starffin threw very hard. We played them tough, but they beat us by one run," said George Aratani.

Setsuo Aratani was loyal to his faithful baseball club and never replaced the veterans with younger players. He went with the same team through the years, and as they passed their prime in the late 1930s, he disbanded the team. The 1927 Aratani team will always be remembered as one of the few company teams to travel across the Pacific to spread goodwill and fellowship, tour the country, expose a multicultural group of players to the country of Japan and, most importantly, play baseball.

In 1932, five years after touring with his father's team, former batboy George Aratani became a varsity shortstop as a freshman on his high school team. That year saw a much-anticipated duel for the state championship between Hoover High School in San Diego and George's Santa Maria team. Scouts lined the fences watching two major-league prospects, Santa Maria pitcher Lester Webber and Hoover first baseman Ted Williams. "Ted was lanky and kind of uncoordinated," George remembered. Webber struck Williams out three times in a row, and Santa Maria went on to win the championship.

Webber was later drafted by the Dodgers, while Williams went on to become a Hall of Famer and one of the greatest hitters in major-league history. George Aratani batted an astonishing .500 for the season, and he and Webber were chosen to work out with the Pittsburgh Pirates. The Pirates came to Paso Robles for spring training, and in remembering Honus Wagner and Paul and Lloyd Waner, George said, "We were lucky to have teaching coaches at the time." All three now grace the halls of Cooperstown. George later ended up playing baseball in Japan at Keio University. Many in baseball circles felt that George was a sure bet for "the Show." He had the size, power and leadership qualities to make it in the major leagues. New York Yankee scout Joe Devine was very interested in George, but no offer was ever made.

JAPANESE AMERICAN WOMEN IN BASEBALL

In the 1920s and 1930s, Japanese American women began to make their mark on the diamond. In addition to their athletic qualities, they displayed a fire and passion that equaled that of the men. The women's teams used a ball that was a little bigger than a men's baseball but smaller than a softball. The pitcher threw overhand, just as in hardball. Alice Hinaga (later Alice Hinaga Taketa) and Asaye Sakamoto gained notoriety by being the only Nisei women to play baseball in the famed Women's Night Ball Association of San Jose. Alice played on merchant teams like the Red and White Stores, Premier Paints, Apricot Growers and Mission Belles as their starting pitcher and cleanup hitter. "Growing up, I would always tag along with my brothers, who played baseball every chance they could get. I guess I got pretty good being around them all the time," said Alice. "At that time, there were no Japanese female baseball teams, so I played with the white American girls. I was the American version of Japanese pitcher Hideo Nomo because I was the only Nisei."

Softball was a very popular offshoot of baseball. Women played in organized church, youth and social leagues. Some even crossed over to play for the highly competitive traveling softball teams. Just like men's baseball, women's baseball and softball sparked new friendships and enabled Nisei women to reach out to new regions and communities. Playing ball enhanced women's self-esteem and provided an outlet for physical conditioning. It also helped to counter the negative image of the subservient, meek woman who could only cook, sew and work in the fields. Alice Hinaga Taketa

Star pitcher Alice Hinaga (front row, far right) was the most outstanding pitcher and hitter on five different merchant teams in the Women's Night Ball Association of San Jose in 1935. These women played with a ball that was bigger than a baseball and smaller than a softball, and they threw overhand. *Courtesy Alice Hinaga Taketa.*

remembered the importance of playing baseball: "I think that our baseball activities prevented a lot of mental anguish. Participation in baseball was a way for me to express myself."

Like the men, women players brought pride to their families and communities. An interesting brother-sister combination occurred in 1937 when Shiro Kawakami was signed to play professional baseball for the Daimai industrial team in Manchuria, China. That same season, his sister Vickie was playing on a merchant team, the Golden State Bakery club in Fresno, California. The following year, two Southern California Nisei women were chosen to play on an integrated softball team that would make a goodwill tour to Japan.

During World War II, women's softball provided a backdrop of normalcy and was as organized as the men's baseball leagues. There were even coed teams. Their games had a much more harmonious feeling and were less intense than league play.

This girls' softball team of the 1920s featured Helen Iwata Tanaka (far right), whose daughter Carolyn would achieve long-lasting notoriety as a softball player, nurse and Vietnam veteran. *Courtesy Carolyn Tanaka.*

One of the most famous and accomplished women's softball players after the war was Nance "The Skipper" Ito. Raised in Denver, Nancy Ito started getting serious about playing ball at the age of thirteen. She loved the game and played it with her brothers and sisters in Brighton, Colorado. She started out in organized ball as a catcher in the Japanese American Softball League and in an integrated women's league, went on to play for the Bank of Denver and competed in the National Softball Tournament. Her extraordinary ability eventually led her to a memorable career with the Orange Lionettes, a Southern California fast-pitch softball team that won four national championships. An outstanding hitter and fielder, she set a record for most doubles in national championship games and made only 10 errors in 1,401 chances. In 1970, Nance played in a world championship representing the United States in a game in Osaka, Japan. She was voted an all-American thirteen times and reached the pinnacle of success in 1982, when she was inducted into the National Softball Hall of Fame in Oklahoma City.

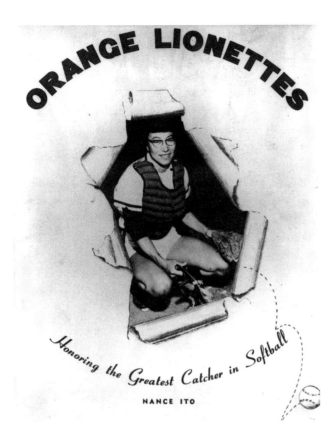

Nance Ito of the Orange Lionettes was a softball legend, achieving all-American honors thirteen times and participating in eighteen national championships in the 1960s and '70s. She has been inducted into the National Softball Hall of Fame. *Courtesy Virginia Ito.*

After her retirement from the Lionettes, Nance went on to manage a professional team in San Diego. "We didn't have any superstars…but everyone gave 110 percent, and we came out on top," she recalled. Throughout her career, her quiet determination and hustle were an inspiration to her teams and communities.

At Manzanar's "A" Field, thousands of fans gathered to watch their hometown heroes from the San Fernando Aces, San Pedro Skippers, Scorpions, Padres, Manza Knights, Oliver's, Has-beens and other organized teams of the camp's twelve leagues. The Aces and Skippers were prewar, semipro powerhouse teams coming into the camp established, while other teams formed in the camps. By the summer of 1942, the camp newspaper, the *Manzanar Press*, was covering nearly one hundred men's and fourteen women's softball teams like the Dusty Chicks, the Modernaires, the Stardusters and the Montebello Gophers. The four primary "A" teams who were considered semipro were the Guadalupe YMBA in Gila River, Arizona; the Florin AC in Jerome, Arkansas; the San Fernando Aces at Manzanar; and the Wakabas at Tule Lake, California. "If it wasn't for the war, I think we could have had a Japanese American major leaguer even before Jackie Robinson," said Tets Furukawa, a pitcher for the Gila River Eagles.

Rosie Kakuuchi played on that field with the Dusty Chicks and was an all-star catcher. "We were so good we even challenged the men to play us and beat them," she said. Rosie's husband, Jack, would enlist and play third base for Camp Grant, an Illinois army team. In 1943, the Camp Grant team would beat the Chicago Cubs 4–3 in an exhibition game.

Kazui "Babe" Oshiki was a tomboy and very proud of it. "Growing up in Hawthorne, California, my parents wanted me to curl my hair and play the piano, but I loved playing baseball," said Oshiki. At sixteen, she tried out for the park league team and was the only non-white girl on the team. Max Factor, the cosmetic company owner, saw the girls play and decided they would be a good advertisement. In 1937, a Los Angeles businessman invited Oshiki on a girls' baseball tour to Japan. "We wanted to challenge Japanese college boys, but the Emperor said 'no,'" she recalled. He was afraid they would lose. So the girls divided into teams, played each other and packed the ball fields. While in high school, Oshiki played for the Orange Lionettes and other respected teams. One weekend, she played on a women's team opening for a men's game. When the men were short one player, they drafted Oshiki. The following morning, the newspaper credited her with a game-winning hit for the men. That is how she got her nickname "Babe."

JAPANESE HALL OF FAMER BOZO WAKABAYASHI

On a small pineapple plantation in Wahiawa, Hawaii, in 1906, the seventh child in a family of eleven was born. Henry Tadashi Wakabayashi was his given name. His parents, who had emigrated from central Japan, let Henry pretty much roam alone, like the other children, and do as he pleased. His folks were busy laboring in the pineapple fields. Down the road from his village was Schofield Barracks, one of the largest military outposts of the United States. Young Henry was attracted to the ball games being played daily on the many diamonds on the compound. He liked the way the soldiers warmed up with two and three bats on their shoulders, and he vowed he would one day do the same. When he finally was strong enough, the soldiers adopted him as one of their own, calling him "Kid" or "Peanut." He became

Nisei legends in the late 1930s, Bozo Wakabayashi and Kaiser Tanaka were the Nisei battery for the Hanshin Tigers in Osaka, Japan. Wakabayashi and Tanaka grew up and competed together in Hawaii. *Courtesy Tad Wakabayashi.*

a familiar sight on the red-dirt fields of Oahu. Later, he went to McKinley High School in Honolulu, one of the best public schools in the territory. The school was noted for its strength in sports, especially football and baseball. Henry's early training with the soldier-ballplayers had toughened him mentally and physically, and he made the varsity teams in both baseball and football in his freshman year. He went on to pitch the school baseball team to two straight championships, and in his last year, he played semipro ball with the Asahi, one of the strongest teams on the islands. During one of the practices in his freshman year of school, his coach couldn't pronounce the multi-syllabic family name, finally shouting out "Bozo" on the spur of the moment. The nickname would stick to Henry the rest of his life.

As related in Chapter 2, in 1928, Bozo was persuaded to join an all-Nisei team from Stockton that was en route to a goodwill tour of Japan. As a result of the tour, he decided to attend college in Japan. Hosei University made a

Kenso Nushida became one of the first professional Japanese American baseball players in 1932 with the Pacific Coast League Sacramento Solons (Senators). Nushida played and coached in the 1935 National Baseball Congress semipro tournament and was an assistant coach for the Alameda-Kono All-Stars on their 1937 tour to Japan, Korea, Manchuria and Harbin, Russia. *Kenichi Zenimura collection.*

strong bid for Bozo, and eventually he qualified after a battery of tests to bring him up to speed in Japanese.

Bozo's debut on the baseball diamond at Hosei came in the opening game of the regular season. The young Nisei pitcher was hammered and took the loss. The second start of his collegiate career was even worse. Suffering two such setbacks in his first two appearances was a huge shock to him. He reminded himself of something a former player who tutored him during his childhood baseball days had said: "You're down and out only when you think you are." Those initial defeats enraged him, and from his third game on, he began pounding opposing pitchers with his hitting ability, many times winning his own games. With Bozo on the mound, Hosei University reached its "golden age" in baseball, attaining three straight championships. In one season, Bozo threw fifteen consecutive games without a rest. That record still stands today, and chances are it will never be matched in Japan.

In 1936, a year after his graduation, Bozo was signed to a professional contract by the Osaka Tigers, Japan's second organized professional baseball club. The Tigers were one of seven teams born within a space of six months for the inauguration of pro ball. It didn't take long for Japan's first two professional teams to battle for the top spot in the nation. The Giants and Tigers had the best players, and they drew capacity crowds. So began the fierce battles of Giants-Tiger competition. To this day, the two teams have the keenest rivalry in Japan. Their epic battles have helped to raise the level of play for all of professional baseball in the country.

Bozo became the Tigers' ace pitcher. Twice (1939 and 1944) he was chosen as the leading pitcher, taking his team to the championship in the latter year. Bozo's claim to fame as a professional was his "seven kinds of pitches." His mixture of pitches and deliveries made him one of the premier pitchers to play major-league baseball in Japan. In his third season with the Tigers, he was elected assistant manager, and the following year he became manager. He was one of the first recorded player-managers in Japan.

Bozo Wakabayashi was very critical of Japanese players for being "too lazy and looking out for themselves"; teamwork, he declared, was "nonexistent." Because of his critical judgment, the style of play began to improve. Bozo also went to bat for the participation of Americans in baseball in Japan. He helped to open up the floodgates for players from his native Hawaii, like Yoshio "Kaiser" Tanaka and Dick Kitamura (who played with the Harlem Globetrotters baseball club). In 1936, catcher Andrew McGalliard came to Japan from Los Angeles. In 1951, Wally Yonamine, from Hawaii, was placed on the all-Japan team.

Bozo captivated the country with his leadership qualities and outgoing personality, but the key to his popularity was his perseverance. After a career that lasted over two decades, in 1964, he became the first American Nisei to be inducted into the hallowed grounds of the Japanese Baseball Hall of Fame.

THE FRESNO ATHLETIC CLUB

During the golden years of Nisei baseball in the 1920s, many semiprofessional "A" teams were establishing themselves. One significant "A" team would compete not only within the Japanese American leagues but would also meet the best teams in the Pacific Coast League and all-stars of the Negro Leagues. This team would travel across the Pacific to Japan several times and even dominate the long-established Big Six university teams. This was a unique team that combined speed, power and technique and even met the challenge of facing some of the players in baseball's Hall of Fame. This team of Nisei all-stars was called the Fresno Athletic Club (FAC).

On March 10, 1924, the all-white Salt Lake City Bees of the PCL traveled to Fresno, California. On this gargantuan-sized team, future Hall of Famer Tony Lazzeri, slugger Lefty O'Doul and a host of other soon-to-be major leaguers filled the roster. Former Red Sox star Duffy Lewis was the manager. Coach Kenichi Zenimura recalled, "Duffy Lewis was managing Salt Lake in those days, and the team was loaded. They had 'Pooshem Up' Tony Lazzeri, who hit sixty home runs; Lefty O'Doul; and a flock of all-stars. We beat them 6–4 behind the pitching of Al Sako." The Nisei used their speed and prowess

on the base paths to best the Bees with critical runs. It was a significant win, especially considering that the Nisei could not even get the ball out of the infield in a game against the Bees the year before. The team also traveled to Japan that year and demonstrated its skills with a 21-7 record.

In 1926, the FAC won the Japanese American state championship and also defeated local college and university teams as, well as the clubs from the Pacific Coast League. That summer, the team traveled to Los Angeles to play the Philadelphia Royal Giants, a team of Negro League stars. The Royal Giants featured Frank Duncan, Biz Mackey and Rap Dixon, all of whom were legends in the Negro Leagues. In an intense battle, the Nisei rallied to win 3–2. Pug Mimura, third baseman for the FAC, recalled, "One of the players hit a screaming line drive so hard that it left seam marks on my palm." These two teams would meet again in Japan the following year at Meiji Jingu Stadium. Both teams had compiled undefeated records against the Big Six universities. It was ironic that in 1927, an African American team and a Japanese American squad were playing for a mythical championship in Tokyo, Japan.

The year 1927 was a unique time in Japanese history. The legacy of imperial Japan was being transferred to a new emperor, Hirohito, who had succeeded his father the year before. There was great enthusiasm and optimism in the country. Baseball was at its high-water mark. The sport provided an important way to connect with the outside world as well as a pastime that fit perfectly with national education and efforts to foster spiritual growth and develop moral character in young men. Even the new emperor left his mark on baseball, offering a beautiful silver cup for the champions of the national high school league. After their triumphal tour of Japan in 1924, the Fresnans were enthusiastic about the possibility of another visit in 1927. They wanted to show again how well they could play, and some players looked forward to visiting family members (Kenichi Zenimura's cousin played for Meiji University in Tokyo). Fresno was willing to pay its own traveling expenses rather than holding out for a financial guarantee.

Opposite, top: The Fresno Athletic Club were the champions of California in 1919–21 and would tour Japan in 1924, 1927 and 1937. *Harvey Iwata collection.*

Opposite, bottom: On July 4, 1926, the Fresno Athletic Club defeated the Seattle Asahi for the Independence Day Championship and the right to tour Japan. Fresno captain Kenichi Zenimura put the visiting Asahi team on the searing sunny side of the field, and as the Seattle team wilted in the heat, FAC won two out of three games. *Courtesy Nori Masuda.*

At Mejii Stadium in Japan, the 1927 Fresno Athletic Club compiled a 40-8-2 record and defeated all of the university squads of the Big Six in Japan. With them are three "ringers" from Fresno State: Charley Hendsch (top, second from right), Jud Simons (top, far right) and Al Hunt (top, fourth from left). *Johnny Nakagawa collection.*

Unbeknownst to the Japanese agents, however, the 1927 Fresno team was loaded with even greater talent than the 1924 squad. The 1927 team was made up of the best Nisei baseball players in California, along with three non-Nisei college-level players. Although the touring team was officially called the Japanese American Baseball Team, the press tended to call it simply Fresno because it was primarily an all-star collection of Japanese Americans who worked in the fields and businesses around Fresno. Most were high school graduates from California and Hawaii. Kenichi Zenimura, Fred Yoshikawa, Ty Miyahara, John Nakagawa and Mike Nakano were all known for their skills, but left fielder Harvey Iwata really picked it up a notch during this tour. Iwata, twenty-seven years old, was the former captain of the Fresno High School championship baseball team and a member of the Japanese League champion FAC squad of 1926. He was an excellent fielder and a speedy base runner. Ty Miyahara, the team's twenty-seven-year-old third baseman, was a former member of the Hawaiian Asahi club. He was a strong hitter and capable infielder. Shortstop Kenichi Zenimura, also twenty-seven, was the manager of the Fresno Athletic Club. A graduate of Mills High School in Honolulu, Zenimura had also been team captain for the Honolulu Asahi. He was a superb infielder and base stealer. Mike Nakano, twenty-one, was the first baseman. A consistent hitter, he was voted the best first baseman of the 1926 California Japanese League. John Nakagawa, twenty-eight, rates a special mention. A center fielder, Nakagawa had pitched and played outfield for the 1926 Fresno High School championship team. He was regarded as the "Nisei Babe Ruth" for the number of home runs he hit. He would hit seven home runs in Japan, including two in one game. He earned honors as the team's best hitter in Japan and was an extraordinary fielder. Another fine outfielder on the Japan tour was Ken Furabayashi. A graduate of Orosi High School, located in a farming town near Fresno, the twenty-year-old Furabayashi was another member of the 1926 FAC championship team. One of the non-Nisei players on the 1927 tour was twenty-four-year-old Charlie Hendsch, a reserve pitcher. A student at Fresno State College, he was captain of both his high school and college teams and played semipro ball in the Taft Oilfield League. As a switch-hitting pitcher, he batted an impressive .400. This squad was truly the team of teams. In sixty-one games, it faced the best amateur and professional players in Japan, compiling a record of fifty wins, nine losses and two ties on a six-month tour that took the squad to Korea, Manchuria and Hawaii. In Hawaii, the team won eight games and lost only one. The five leading hitters in Japan were Harvey Iwata (.333), Ty Miyahara (.323), Kenichi Zenimura (.295), Mike Nakano (.385) and John Nakagawa (.388). The Fresno Athletic Club's exploits demonstrated the quality of Japanese American baseball and helped to elevate the play of the game in Japan—a primary purpose of summer barnstorming. Teams such as the FAC and the Philadelphia Royal Giants provided a snapshot of the baseball competence that Nisei and black players shared with their white counterparts at a time when racial divisions created separate but equal leagues in the United States, and there was little chance for interracial play. The 1927 Fresno squad added a twist by including three outstanding white players on their tour—two catchers and a pitcher—whose style of play helped to provide essential tools for Japan's improvement program. As showmen, the FAC players gave their audiences something to "ooh" and "aah" over. They were continually bashing the ball and scampering on the bases while stifling the opposition. They demonstrated classy baseball as well as character. They visited Korea and Manchuria and shared their baseball savvy over a wider area of the Japanese Empire than any previous

In 1927, Biz Mackey, Rap Dixon and Frank Duncan led the Philadelphia Royal Giants, a team of Negro League all-stars, through Japan, China, the Philippines, Australia and Hawaii. *Courtesy Kazuo Sayama.*

touring baseball team, exposing Japanese players and fans to a superior amateur baseball team model. In playing a sixty-one-game schedule and winning 80 percent of its contests, the FAC achieved a feat matched by no other amateur team in the thirty-two-year history of international baseball exchanges. Ironically, it was Fresno's behavior on Japan's baseball diamonds that demonstrated the essence of *showa*, a political ideal of that era in Japan, a practice of civilized peace and harmony.

BABE RUTH AND LOU GEHRIG BARNSTORM TO FRESNO

On a cool October morning in that same year of 1927, thousands of fans eagerly awaited the arrival of a train at the Fresno station. As the train pulled in, young and old alike converged on the last car, from which they knew the baseball stars would exit. Monsignor J.J. Crowley led hundreds of kids as they prepared to welcome the great "Sultan of Swat" and "The Iron Horse," Babe Ruth and Lou Gehrig. The mighty Yankees had just swept the World Series, and this was the first opportunity for West Coast fans to see the two megastars in the flesh. Paul Carmello remembered, "I was on the train selling newspapers and went to the back, and there was Lou Gehrig and Babe Ruth waiting to leave. Babe called me over and gave me a quarter for one of my newspapers. I thanked him and was ready to leave, and he told me to go out the door next to them. I went out, and the crowd screamed, thinking it was Ruth and Gehrig coming out. I could hear Ruth laughing as I jumped down and took off running."

The appearance of the two living legends was an epic moment for the small California city. Ruth and Gehrig were taken by motorcade to Fireman's Park. Awaiting them were the local major leaguers and Pacific Coast stars who had been chosen to play in an exhibition game with the Yankee greats. Four of the all-stars were local Nisei ballplayers. They represented the epitome of athletic power, speed and finesse. One of them was John Nakagawa, the "Nisei Babe Ruth," who once hit a four-hundred-foot shot into the right-field bleachers of Honolulu Stadium against the Navy Nine. Nakagawa was always a threat to hit one out. He batted over .400 against the all-stars of the Negro Leagues and the Tokyo Giants traveling squad. Kenichi Zenimura, the coach, captain and manager of the semipro Nisei club, was there along with Fred Yoshikawa, an all-star catcher (and a city golf champion) with a cannon for an arm. Harvey Iwata was considered the Ted Williams of the team. He consistently batted over the .400 mark wherever he played, and strong competition only made him better.

Ruth and Gehrig represented a team that many say was the greatest ever to take the field. The Yankees had faced Pittsburgh in the World Series, and in their first practice session at Forbes Field, Gehrig slugged one ball after another over the distant fences. The Pirates sat in the grandstand, watching in awed silence. Some say that they were beaten before they even took the field. They were probably right. During batting practice, a bell was rung every time a ball was hit over the wall. When the Pirates took batting practice, the bell went off perhaps two times. When the Yankees stepped up to the plate, the constant "dings" sounded like a cable car going by in San Francisco. Ruth and Gehrig were the unparalleled stars of a team on which the collective batting average was .307. Ruth was thirty-two years old and at the pinnacle of his career. In 1927, he batted .356, smashed a record sixty home runs and collected 164 RBIs. Larrupin' Lou was only twenty-four but had already blossomed into one of the game's greatest stars. He hit for a .373 average that season while hitting forty-seven home runs and driving in 175 runs. He was named the league's most valuable player.

Ruth and Gehrig were in great public demand after the 1927 World Series, and Christy Walsh, Ruth's business manager, organized the barnstorming tour so that fans across the country could come out and see them. In those days, major-league

Above: Monsignor J.J. Crowley and young Jett Walker got the once-in-a-lifetime chance to meet baseball immortality in Lou Gehrig (left) and Babe Ruth (right of center) during their 1927 eight-city tour of California. It was the only time their West Coast fans had the chance to watch these two baseball icons perform. *Courtesy Stephen L. Brown, Imag Live; photograph by Claude Lavel.*

Opposite, top: Lou Gehrig and Babe Ruth autographed a dinner ticket for Fresno State pitcher Charley Hendsch. This was during the same year that Hendsch toured Japan with the Fresno Athletic Club. *Courtesy David Hendsch.*

Opposite, bottom: This 1927 signed commemorative barnstorming photo of Babe Ruth and Lou Gehrig sold for twenty-five cents during their eight-city California tour. *Courtesy Fred Yoshikawa.*

baseball was still an east-of-the-Mississippi proposition, and most Americans knew Ruth and Gehrig only through stories and pictures in newspapers and silent newsreels. Traveling any great distance to see a major-league team like the Yankees, Cardinals or Pirates was a luxury beyond the reach of millions of enthusiastic baseball fans.

During the tour, the two Yankee stars played on opposing teams—the Bustin' Babes and the Larrupin' Lous. The teams were staffed by local professional and semipro players along the tour route. The tour gradually made its way across the country, playing day after day in sold-out ballparks filled with starstruck fans. Nearly a quarter of a million fans in eighteen states came out to see the Yankee stars shine. When the tour reached San Francisco, the exhibition game drew thirteen thousand fans. Gehrig hit a home run that day, but Ruth was shut out, much to the disappointment of the crowd. The tour went on to Oakland, Marysville, Stockton, Sacramento, San Jose, Fresno, Santa Barbara, San Diego and Los Angeles. Ruth batted .616 on the tour and hit twenty home runs. Gehrig batted .618 with thirteen home runs. Legend has it that Ruth hit one shot that went between the pitcher's legs and kept on rising, finally clearing the center-field fence.

In Fresno, the *Fresno Bee* was billing the scheduled exhibition as a meeting between the legends of one game and Fresno's new crop of baseball stars. Among the players who filled out the teams were Alex Metzler, an outfielder for the Chicago White Sox; future major leaguer Howard Craighead, a pitching star for the Oakland Oaks; Moose Cano, a pitcher with the Hollywood All-Stars; Kenichi Zenimura, captain of the Fresno Athletic Club; and Fred Yoshikawa, Harvey Iwata and John Nakagawa of the FAC. Five thousand exuberant fans filled Fireman's Park to see the contest, the largest crowd ever to attend a baseball game there. Although Lou Gehrig did not connect for a home run during the game, he socked one over the left center-field fence during batting practice and drove two over the fence in deep center. In the first inning, Ruth took a Howard Craighead fastball over the right-field fence. Ruth's prodigious drive cleared the fence, 410 feet from home plate, by a big margin. In addition to hitting, Ruth seized the chance to display his pitching expertise. In the third inning, his pitcher went to pieces, allowing five runs to cross the plate before there were any outs. Ruth strolled over to the mound. He made four pitches and received credit for pitching a full inning when Jackie Kohl, the second baseman for the Bustin' Babes, snagged a line drive over second, touched the base and tossed to third for a triple play to end the inning!

The ball game went on the rocks in the ninth inning. Hundreds of kids flocked onto the infield, surrounding Gehrig and Ruth and clamoring for

Lou Gehrig and Babe Ruth competed with the all-stars of the Twilight League at Fireman's Park in Fresno, California, on October 29, 1927. Gehrig and his Nisei teammates defeated the Babe 13–3 in a game that featured a Babe Ruth home run, the Babe pitching and even a triple play. *Kenichi Zenimura collection.*

autographs. The crowd on the field got so big that the game had to be called with two down in the ninth. Lou's team hammered the Babes 13–3. Gehrig was happy with the outcome of the game, and especially with having the Nisei on his side. Kenichi Zenimura went one for two and had a stolen base. John Nakagawa was one for two with a steal and caught a Ruth fly for a putout. Fred Yoshikawa had a double to score a run. Although this might have been the first encounter with Nisei players for Babe Ruth and Lou Gehrig, one afternoon at the ballpark would give them a better understanding of and respect for Japanese American ballplayers. Kenichi Zenimura would recall:

> *Lou Gehrig was playing for us and Babe Ruth for the Sun Maids (sponsor of the Bustin' Babes). The first time I got up, I got a single. I was very fast*

and took my usual big lead on first. Ruth laughed at me and said, "Hey son, are you taking too much of a lead?" I said, "No." He called for the pitcher to pick me off. The pitcher threw, and I slipped behind Ruth. He was looking around to tag me, and I was already on the sack. I think this made him mad. He called for the ball again. This time he was blocking the base, and he swung his arm around, thinking I would slide the same way. But this time I slipped through his legs, and he was looking behind. The fans cheered. Ruth said, "If you do that to me again, I'll pick you up and use you as a bat, you runt."

Ruth's pique was short-lived. After the game, the *Fresno Bee* took a picture of Zenimura, Iwata, Yoshikawa and Nakagawa with Ruth and Gehrig.

It was perhaps as a result of this encounter that Ruth learned about the passion for baseball in Japan. "I got a call from Japan to see if I could get Ruth to the island and play for a $40,000 guarantee," Kenichi Zenimura remembered. "I contacted Ruth, and he said he would go for $60,000. It was much too much then, but a few years later, they went and made a big hit."

RINGERS OF NISEI BASEBALL

Amid all the dynamics of Japanese American baseball, there have been a number of Caucasian ballplayers and other individuals who have been officially adopted by Nisei teams and players. One of the earliest was former major-league catcher Tubby Spencer. Tubby started his major-league career with the St. Louis Browns in 1905 and played for the Boston Red Sox in 1909. After five years in the big leagues, Spencer, an admitted alcoholic, dropped out of baseball for a year. Traded by the Red Sox to the Phillies, he played a few games with Philadelphia in 1911 and then disappeared again. He rode the rails as a hobo and was homeless for five years before deciding to try to make another comeback. He tried out for the Detroit Tigers and made the team in 1916. He responded by batting .370 in nineteen games and continued playing for the Tigers until 1918, when he retired.

Tubby's playing days were over, but his coaching duties were just beginning. He migrated to Los Angeles and befriended the Los Angeles Nippon squad. Soon he found a new life as Coach Spencer, becoming one of the first white

Former major leaguer Tubby Spencer (top, fourth from left) coached the Los Angeles Nippon in 1929. A fascinating character, Spencer played sporadically for the St. Louis Browns, Boston Red Sox and Philadelphia Phillies between 1905 and 1911. An alcoholic, Spencer disappeared and became a hobo, riding the rails, for five years. Then, in 1916, he reappeared, hitting .370 in nineteen games for the Detroit Tigers. Spencer played two more years with the Tigers, retiring after the 1918 season with a .225 lifetime batting average. *Tom Tomiyama collection.*

major-league coaches of a Nisei ball club. In 1931, the Nippon traveled to Japan, where they compiled a 20-5 record. Doc Crandall, a former New York Giants pitcher, assisted Spencer in coaching the team.

One of the players on the Nippon team, Peter Kondo, became a quadriplegic after a traffic accident in which a telephone pole fell and crushed his car. Later, Peter was interned at the Manzanar Concentration Camp in California. By chance, one of the ballplayers recognized Peter in the camp hospital. The internees surprised Peter with a special ceremony, honoring him at the camp baseball diamond with Peter Kondo Day. He later went on to achieve recognition as a fine painter.

Besides Tubby Spencer, other Caucasian players who became involved with Japanese American baseball in the pre–World War II years included Bucky Harris, Doc Crandall and Gordon Ford, all with the L.A. Nippon. In the early 1920s, the Stockton Yamato had Mike Matteoni and Hugh McMurray on their roster, and as mentioned earlier, the Fresno Athletic Club took three non-Nisei players with them on their tour to Japan in 1927.

One of them, Charlie Hendsch, was a standout at Fresno State in both baseball and football. He still holds the record at Fresno State for the longest drop-kick field goal at fifty-one yards.

In 1937, the Alameda-Kono All-Stars traveled to Japan, Korea and Manchuria. To ensure a strong staff, they recruited George Davis, Paul Allison, Marion Alleruzo and Norman Riggs. These college players were sought out for both their playing skills and their tough mental capacity.

Postwar notables who became involved in Japanese American baseball include singing-cowboy sensation Jack Hannah, who pitched for George Omachi's team in 1953 when the Tokyo Giants came to Fresno. Omachi was a legend in the Fresno area as a coach, scout and player. "George and I were both ballplayers before we coached. He was a great human being who impacted many ballplayers," said Hannah. Another adopted Nisei was Bobby Cox, later manager of the Atlanta Braves, who once convinced Omachi that his mother was Japanese, qualifying him to play second base in a tournament. Hall of Famer Tom Seaver played in a Nisei baseball game in the late 1950s with George Omachi as his catcher. Still another major leaguer, Rex Hudler, assisted George Omachi with coaching before going on to play for the Yankees, Orioles, Expos and Cardinals. In 1993, Rex played in Japan and helped the Yakult Swallows win the Japanese championship.

Jackie Robinson's Nisei Teammates

Until 1947, when Jackie Robinson broke the color barrier, it wasn't possible for a nonwhite ballplayer to play in the majors. For the Nisei of the 1920s and 1930s, playing with the pros meant finding ways to compete outside of organized baseball. In addition to the exhibition games already described, there were a number of encounters between Nisei players and well-known present and future major leaguers.

One future major-league star who played with and against Nisei players was Jackie Robinson. As a youth, Jackie would get together with Shig Kawai and the rest of the local sandlot ballplayers on a dusty lot in West Pasadena. "We would just play for the fun of it, and it was our special baseball gang," said Shig. Later, Shig and Jackie would be football teammates at Pasadena Junior College.

Jackie and Nisei Shig Takayama were teammates on the Pasadena Junior College baseball team. This squad was a multiracial group that battled racism on and off the fields. Road trips to other regions became exercises in humility as the team tried to find a hotel that would accept one black and one Japanese player along with their white teammates. Registering the white players was never a problem, but when it came to Shig and Jackie, the team's home on the road often depended on how much business a hotel could stand to lose because of its racial policy. If the hotel wouldn't accept his nonwhite players, coach John Thurman would pull the whole team. When they did find rooms, Jackie and Shig were usually bunked as roommates in small rooms in the back of the hotel. Shig remembered their routine: "So Jackie and I got ready to sleep, and we said good night. I turned out the light and heard him move around. I looked over, and I could see him kneeling beside his bed, praying, with a tear coming down his cheek."

In 1937, Lefty Nishijima, a pitcher for Santa Maria Junior College, squared off against Jackie in a game against Pasadena. Lefty faced Jackie three times and gave up two home runs to the gifted athlete. Later, Lefty said wryly, "I am very happy that I helped Jackie Robinson's career. I gave him a lot of confidence. He took advantage of the short right-field fence." Tashi Hori, Lefty's catcher, remembered, "Jackie got a single and was on first base. I knew he was fast, but he did not steal on us. Later, he left the game, and Shig Takayama took his spot."

Ten years later, Jackie crossed over into the major leagues and opened up the doors for all people of color. He was a pioneer who gave hope to all the "other Americans" who wanted only a chance to compete on a level playing field. In the process, he more than lived up to his own saying: "A life is not important except in the impact it has on other lives."

The inspiring legacy of Jackie Robinson is mirrored in the pioneering exploits of second-generation Japanese Americans. Throughout this chapter, there have been many examples of Nisei ballplayers who had the opportunity to test their mettle against their professional and major-league peers. Although they remained in leagues of their own, they seized every chance to demonstrate their skills against the toughest competition. In the process, these Nisei ballplayers elevated their game, proved that they could compete at the highest level and helped to begin the long process of bucking the barriers that stood between Japanese Americans and full participation in American life.

Chapter 6
DESERT DIAMONDS BEHIND
BARBED WIRE

*Without baseball, camp life would have been miserable...It was humiliating and
demeaning being incarcerated in our own country.*
—George Omachi

On December 7, 1941, World War II came to U.S. territory and changed
the lives of Japanese Americans forever. Within a year, more than
120,000 people of Japanese descent were forcibly relocated into cramped,
prison-like concentration camps. Later in the war, on battlefields in the
Philippines, Japanese soldiers looking to insult their American foes would
commonly scream from their foxholes, "To hell with Babe Ruth!" Across the
Pacific, Japanese Americans confined behind barbed wire were passionately
playing the game that Ruth made famous. Even as white America held them
suspect, they held fast to the national game. Baseball had become deeply
ingrained in Japanese American culture; it was part of the heritage of Issei
and Nisei alike. Moreover, during this incarceration, baseball represented
salvation and hope for thousands who needed a positive reminder of home
life as it used to be and might be again.

BANISHMENT

In 1942, the United States was at war with Germany and Italy as well Japan. Yet the federal government saw fit to declare only Japanese Americans enemy aliens. Even before the attack on Pearl Harbor—when the United States and Japan were still at peace—Japanese Americans had been singled out for special attention. On July 25, 1941, a presidential order froze Japanese assets in the United States, causing a run on Japanese banks. On November 12, fifteen Japanese American businessmen and community leaders in Los Angeles were picked up in a raid by the FBI.

After Pearl Harbor, anti-Japanese hysteria grew, fueled by a swell of negative reports in the media. A *Los Angeles Times* editorial on February 2, 1942, was a chilling example of the way most media outlets portrayed Japanese Americans:

> *A viper is nonetheless a viper wherever the egg is hatched. So a Japanese-American born of Japanese parents nurtured upon Japanese traditions, living in a transparent Japanese-American atmosphere and thoroughly inoculated with Japanese ideals, notwithstanding his nominal brand of accidental citizenship, almost inevitably, and with the rarest exceptions, grows up a Japanese and not an American in his ideas and is menacing unless hamstrung. Thus, while it might cause injustice to a few to treat them all as potential enemies...I cannot escape the conclusion that such treatment should be accorded to each and all of them while we are at war with their race.*

That same month, under Franklin Delano Roosevelt's Executive Order 9066, the U.S. government ordered the mass eviction and incarceration of all Japanese Americans living on the West Coast. German and Italian immigrants remained free.

In mid-February, a congressional committee held hearings on "National Defense Migration" in Seattle, Portland, San Francisco and Los Angeles. During these hearings, there was overwhelming resistance to a proposal by General Dewitt to include German and Italian aliens in the evacuation process. A San Francisco lawyer, Chauncey Tramutolo, focused on the potential plight of baseball great Joe DiMaggio's parents. When World War II broke out, Giuseppe and Rosalie DiMaggio, who had emigrated from Sicily at the turn of the century, still had not become American citizens. Rather, they were classified as resident aliens. Giuseppe was in a particularly gray situation because he was a fisherman who made his living off the waters of San Francisco, a forbidden zone for aliens living in Martinez,

California. Nevertheless, Tramutolo told the congressmen that to evacuate the DiMaggios would "in view of the splendid family they had reared and their unquestioned loyalty, present, I am sure you will agree with me, a serious situation. I believe it would be destructive and have a tendency to lower morale which all of us are building if information should reach those in the armed forces that their relatives have an order to move out of this area because, unfortunately, they are not citizens." Of course, in the congressional hearings, there were no major-league Japanese American baseball players like Joltin' Joe DiMaggio to serve as silent witnesses.

Within days after the issuance of Executive Order 9066, Japanese Americans were removed from their homes on the West Coast, neighborhood by neighborhood. Detainees spent much of the spring and summer of 1942 in so-called assembly centers. Assembly centers were hastily erected quarters located throughout California and the West at fairgrounds, racetracks and similar facilities. Although conditions varied from center to center, they were generally poor, as might be expected given the haste with which they were put up. Residents complained of overcrowding, shoddy construction and communal showers and outhouses. The worst indignity of all was being housed in the odorous horse stables and animal stalls in the racetracks and fairgrounds of Tanforan, Santa Anita and Fresno. Security was very tight; military police patrolled the perimeters and regulated visitors, while internal police held roll calls and enforced curfews.

ASSEMBLY CENTER BASEBALL

With the roundup of Japanese Americans and their confinement in assembly centers, the government took away their freedom, their constitutional rights, their radios, their cameras and their religion. In the case of the Issei, the government was even against them speaking in their native language. Ironically, Uncle Sam did not deny Japanese Americans the opportunity to play baseball. Almost immediately, the detainees set to work developing diamonds and erecting backstops. In Pullywap and Portland, Marysville and Tanforan, Fresno and Santa Anita—in fact, wherever Japanese Americans were confined—teams began to organize, and baseball flourished.

Inside the assembly centers, most families were reflecting sadly on the homes, cars, furniture, refrigerators and heirlooms that were being

The Florin baseball squad was the Fresno Assembly Center (FAC) Class A champions in 1942. Many FAC players began their internment in Fresno, where their sleeping quarters were animal stalls that had been hosed out with water. *Courtesy Bill Tsukamoto.*

The second of three baseball diamonds to be designed by Kenichi Zenimura was constructed at the Fresno Assembly Center in 1942, where this FAC team gathered for a photo. The first Zenimura diamond had been in Fresno in 1919, and the third would constructed be in Gila River, Arizona, in 1943. More than five thousand internees would reside at the Fresno Assembly Center. *Courtesy Nori Masuda.*

sold for ten cents on the dollar. They could bring into the centers only what they could carry in two suitcases. Even as they tried to adjust to their new living quarters, the government was hastily preparing ten permanent camps in desert wastelands. The forced migration into the centers and camps was a rough transition, abrupt and shattering. For people whose culture stressed personal decorum and hygiene and truly placed a premium on privacy, the indignities of assembly center and camp life were a huge painful hardship.

One of the first problems facing the internees was how to establish a sense of normalcy in the face of totally disrupted patterns of life. Cultural, recreational and work activities took on tremendous importance. There were schools for the children, and many adults employed by the government earned standard G.I. wages. The top wage, nineteen dollars per month, went to doctors and other professionals. Teachers, secretaries and other support staff earned sixteen dollars, while laborers received twelve.

Baseball played a major role in the effort to create a degree of continuity in the disrupted lives of the internees. At the Fresno Assembly Center, there was nothing but the fairgrounds. In May 1942, Kenichi Zenimura looked out at the barren landscape and knew exactly what needed to be done. "Every time my dad went some place, if there was no baseball park, he'd make one," said his son Howard.

"Zeni had everything for a baseball diamond plan in his mind," recalled Moon Kurima, who managed and pitched for the Florin Athletic Club in the assembly center. "He lined up tractors, lumber and carpenters, and we started to work on the grounds. Within a week, everything was ready." Three leagues were formed: a six-team "A" semipro division, a high school–level "B" circuit and a junior high "C" level division. Many of the better draft-age players were already in the armed forces, so Kurima and the other managers had to patch together teams from the available talent, mostly aging veterans and inexperienced high school kids.

Through a friend in Sacramento, Moon Kurima sent for his team's uniforms and equipment, which he had the foresight to collect and put into storage before the evacuation. Kurima was an established star whose blazing fastball and pinpoint control had made him one of the most dominant pitchers in prewar Nisei baseball. In 1937, he threw an amazing one-hitter for the Elk Grove American Legion squad against the Grass Valley American Legion team, striking out twenty-one batters! With Kurima at the helm (and on the mound), the Florin club quickly established itself as the team to beat in the assembly center's "A" league. Florin went undefeated in thirteen games, with

Moon Kurima was one of the best pitchers to come out of Northern California. Once, while pitching for the Oak Grove American Legion team against Grass Valley in 1937, Moon struck out twenty-one batters and hurled a one-hitter while pitching his team to a victory. *Courtesy Herb Kurima.*

Kurima winning ten. In a contest before three thousand spectators—more than half the center's population—Florin beat an all-star team managed by Kenichi Zenimura, 7–2, behind Kurima's six-hit pitching.

The B-league title was captured by the Fresno Bee club. The Fresno team included Kenichi Zenimura's sons, fifteen-year-old Howard and thirteen-year-old Harvey, both of whom went on to play big-league Japanese ball for the Hiroshima Carp in the 1950s. The team also boasted future major-league scout George

Hatsuo Omachi, or "Hats," as most people called him. George summed up the importance of baseball during the internment: "Without baseball, camp life would have been miserable. There was no torture or anything like that, but it was humiliating and demeaning being incarcerated in your own country."

Behind Barbed Wire: Baseball in the Concentration Camps

In October 1942, the internees of the assembly centers were again uprooted and assigned to one of the ten permanent camps that were scattered throughout barren regions in California, Arizona, Utah, South Dakota, Wyoming, Colorado, Arkansas and Idaho. The internees were escorted by soldiers and herded onto trains with covered windows that took them to their destinations in desert wastelands and swamps.

Yoshino Hasegawa was ten years old when her family was taken to the Poston, Arizona camp. "When we first arrived in the desert, I was really frightened and did not know what awaited us," she recalled. "One evening I was with my friend next to the barbed wire, and we could see on the horizon a lightning storm. It kept coming closer and really started to thunder and flash...I am a Christian and believe in God, and after witnessing that magnificent storm in the desert, I knew he was with us and we would be all right. I never was afraid of camp life after that experience."

The triple-threat combination of Jim, Yosh and Bill Tsukamoto from Florin, California, led their Military Intelligence Service (MIS) team against a team headed by Spurgeon "Spud" Chandler of the New York Yankees in 1944. Bill tripled off Chandler, and the MIS team won 4–2. *Courtesy Mas Masuda.*

The internees' new homes would be sagebrush and sand. But after resettling barracks twenty feet wide and one hundred feet long, one of the first tasks they undertook was building baseball diamonds.

George Omachi catches for the Denson All-Stars in a game with the Rohwer All-Stars in Jerome, Arkansas, in 1943. Omachi would become a major-league scout who played a pivotal role in the development of several major-league stars, including Tom Seaver and the Atlanta Braves' Bobby Cox. *Courtesy Fred Kumagai.*

Too close to call. George Omachi dives to make a tag in the 1942 all-star game between Denson and Rohwer in Jerome, Arkansas, in 1942. *Courtesy Fred Kumagai.*

The majority of the group from the Fresno Assembly Center was sent to Jerome, Arkansas. George Omachi recalled, "I was on the clean-up community, so I was one of the last to leave the Fresno Assembly Center. I stayed behind about a month or six weeks. By the time I got to Jerome, they already had a baseball stadium." At Tule Lake, located on a dry lake bottom in the northeastern part of the state of California, volunteers cleared rocks and seashells from one area to make a diamond. At Manzanar, in the California desert near Death Valley, teams took turns going up to the hills in a dump truck looking for decomposed granite. They would lay the granite down in the bleacher and dugout sections of the ball field, as well as on the infield, to cut down on all the dust that was stirred up during games. San Fernando Aces catcher Barry Tamura worked for the camp fire department, and he saw to it that the field was well watered by conducting frequent fire drills on the diamond.

All ten camps developed baseball diamonds, leagues and teams. The four primary "A" teams that were considered semipro were the Guadalupe YMBA (Young Men's Buddhist Association) at Gila River, the Florin Athletic Club at Jerome, the San Fernando Aces at Manzanar and the Wakabas at Tule Lake.

Re-creating organized baseball in the camps required dedication and ingenuity. "We ordered jerseys from Sears-Roebuck, and one of the fellows stenciled in the name," related the gravel-voiced Hugo Nishimoto, who managed the Placer-Hillman squad in the Tule Lake championship of 1943. "The pants were potato sacks that came from the farm. They were heavy cotton, bleached white. Two or three ladies sewed them on for us, and they looked real professional." Another Tule Lake team, the Wakabas, removed the canvas-covered ticking from their government-issued mattresses and had custom shirts and pants made. At Topaz, Utah, red lettering was stenciled on uniforms that were also made of mattress ticking.

Once teams were organized, passions ran high among spectators and players alike. As was true before the war, betting on games was common among the Nisei. Harry Tamura remembered three old men who attended every game at Manzanar and bet so much money that none trusted any of the others with the cash. Every inning, a different member of the trio would hold the stakes. At the time, the San Fernando Aces were enjoying a winning streak that would lead to the 1943 camp championship. "We were scheduled to play the weakest team in the league, the Sacramento Solons," said the angular Tamura, a retired gardener, whose voice rose and fell emphatically as he told the story. "One of the old men who always bet on us was very happy, and he told everyone that he would pay three-to-one odds. What he didn't know was

This Jerome, Arkansas team, along with those from Gila River, Arizona, and Tule Lake and Manzanar, California, was a powerhouse of "A" baseball in 1944. Many of the Jerome players were from either Fresno or Florin, California. *Courtesy Herb Kurima.*

This 1943 championship team from the Manzanar detention facility was involved in one of the most memorable incidents of the era. In a 1944 game against the Poston team from Arizona, a questionable call by the umpires started one of the biggest fan and player brawls in camp history. *Courtesy Pete Mitsui.*

Thousands watch as Bill Tsukamoto awaits the pitch at the Jerome, Arkansas detention camp. Since the alternative was living in a twenty- by one-hundred-foot barracks that was divided into quadrants with no privacy, most internees chose to play or watch baseball. *Courtesy Mas Masuda.*

that the Solons had recruited a pitcher from Japan named Horimoto, and he was hotter than a firecracker that day. We couldn't touch him and we lost, and that old man had to pay big bucks. He was white. He wouldn't eat anything, and he looked like he'd been kicked by a horse."

At Tule Lake, one large segment of the camp came from in and around California's Sacramento Valley and was dark-complected from farming in the intense valley sun. The other portion of the population consisted of people from Oregon and Washington. Bill Matsumoto recalled:

> *It was a strange mixture of regional people, and we didn't hit it off too well socially. The Oregon or Washington people would call us black Californians or something, and a fight would start. So we weren't on very good terms. More than one time we got chased out of the ballpark because the fans got so carried away. The cardinal rule was that we would talk back to the fans. There would be a close play and one of them would say, "He was out!" and one of us would say something like, "No he wasn't, you dumbbell!" and that would start a fight. They would come after you with bats. There were times we just had to go home and run like hell.*

Kenichi Zenimura's Field of Dreams

With the arrival of the internees at Gila River and Poston Camps I, II and III in Arizona, the camps became the third- and fourth-largest cities in the state overnight. More than thirteen thousand internees filed into the Gila River Camp II in Butte. The camp's buildings were designed with double roofs to help ventilate the barracks and provide some protection from the intense desert heat. The internees shredded sheets and used the strips to stuff the cracks in the floor in order to keep out the clouds of dust that would enter the rooms during the harsh windstorms. On the exterior of the housing units, reflective white sheet rock was used to reduce the searing heat.

Among the internees at Gila River were Kenichi Zenimura; his wife, Kiyoko; and their sons, Howard and Harvey. Later, Kiyoko reflected on Kenichi's anger over having been sent to Gila River instead of Jerome, Arkansas, where his ball-playing peers were sent. "He left his suitcases packed for two weeks. He didn't even bother opening them," she recalled. But one day Kenichi looked out from Barrack 13C, Block 28, on the corner of the detention facility, at the vast desert surrounding the camp. For most, the sagebrush, rocks and cactus were a vision of hopelessness and desolation. For Zenimura, the scene meant the possibility of another ballpark. Kenichi had already built the Japanese ballpark on the west side of Fresno bordering the city dump in the early 1920s. The Fresno Assembly Center was his second diamond, and now Gila River became his crown jewel.

Howard Zenimura was there the day the men began clearing away sagebrush from the desert floor. "Right near our block was an open space, so we started digging out the sagebrush with shovels," Howard said many years later. "Pretty soon, people came by to ask us what we were doing. We told them we were building a ballpark, and then everybody was out there with their shovels clearing that space. We piled up the brush and burned it, and my dad somehow got a bulldozer to level the ground."

Not content with simply having a cleared space to play, Zenimura and the other men liberated every second four-by-four from the barbed-wire fence surrounding the camp until they had enough to build a frame for the backstop. Then they took thick padding that was used to keep wet cement from drying too quickly and hung it over the frame to provide a cushion for errant fastballs and other wild pitches. (The only catch was having to pick up all the pads each day and check for rattlesnakes or scorpions.)

Next, they worked on the mound and infield, scraping the top layer and sifting out rocks and pebbles. One of the internees who helped was James "Step"

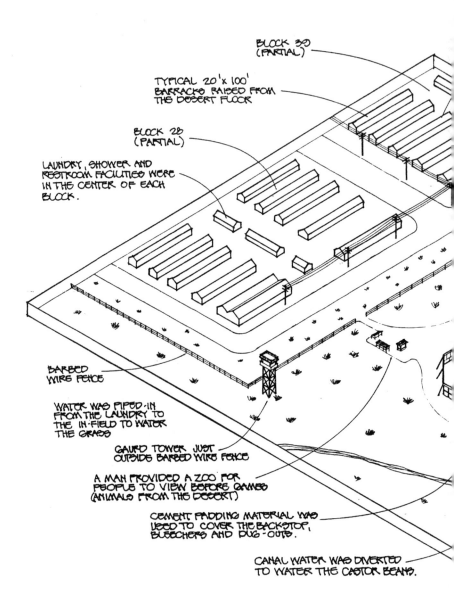

BLOCK 30
(PARTIAL)

TYPICAL 20' x 100'
BARRACKS RAISED FROM
THE DESERT FLOOR

BLOCK 28
(PARTIAL)

LAUNDRY, SHOWER AND
RESTROOM FACILITIES WERE
IN THE CENTER OF EACH
BLOCK.

BARBED
WIRE FENCE

WATER WAS PIPED-IN
FROM THE LAUNDRY TO
THE IN-FIELD TO WATER
THE GRASS

GAURD TOWER JUST
OUTSIDE BARBED WIRE FENCE

A MAN PROVIDED A ZOO FOR
PEOPLE TO VIEW BEFORE GAMES
(ANIMALS FROM THE DESERT)

CEMENT PADDING MATERIAL WAS
USED TO COVER THE BACKSTOP,
BLEECHERS AND DUG-OUTS.

CANAL WATER WAS DIVERTED
TO WATER THE CASTOR BEANS.

The third diamond to be designed and constructed by Kenichi Zenimura—Zenimura Field, Block 28, 13C in Gila River, Arizona—was one of the finest ballparks among those at the ten detention camps. *Courtesy Sidney Mukai.*

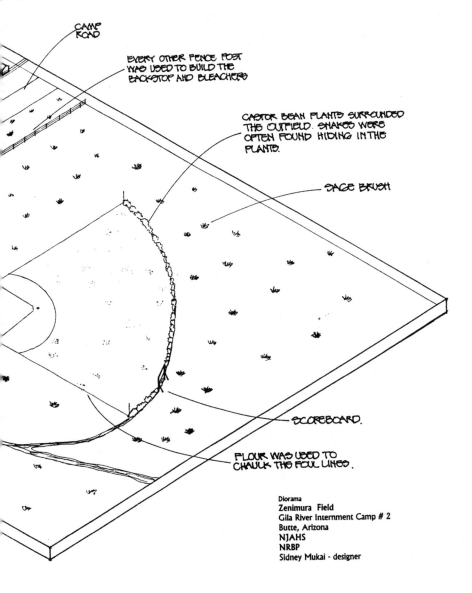

...CKS WERE WHITE
...HITE WALLS AND
...B ROOFS

CAMP ROAD

EVERY OTHER FENCE POST WAS USED TO BUILD THE BACKSTOP AND BLEACHERS

CASTOR BEAN PLANTS SURROUNDED THE OUTFIELD. SNAKES WERE OFTEN FOUND HIDING IN THE PLANTS.

SAGE BRUSH

SCOREBOARD.

FLOUR WAS USED TO CHALK THE FOUL LINES.

Diorama
Zenimura Field
Gila River Internment Camp # 2
Butte, Arizona
NJAHS
NRBP
Sidney Mukai - designer

Known as the "Dean of the Diamond," Kenichi Zenimura is considered to be the most versatile of the Nisei ballplayers. He was a multi-position player, coach, captain, manager and organizer. He actively played ball until he was fifty-five years old. Many have called Zenimura the father of Japanese American baseball. *Kenichi Zenimura collection.*

Captain Kenichi Zenimura (second row, left) pictured with his 1924 H.E. Jaynes & Sons Twilight League team. Zenimura and his Nisei teammates proved that, even in otherwise an all-white league, talent transcends prejudice. Zenimura played for Al's Club and played for and managed the Fresno Athletic Club in this high-powered semipro league. *Kenichi Zenimura collection.*

Tomooka, a hard-hitting outfielder whose Guadalupe YMBA squad would win the camp's inaugural "A" championship. (His nickname stemmed from his foot speed, or perhaps the lack thereof.) Along with the Zenimuras, James got down on his hands and knees to seek out every pebble before the internees diverted water from a nearby irrigation ditch and flooded the infield to harden and pack it down. Then they took a three-hundred-foot water line from the laundry room and made a spigot at the back end of the pitcher's mound so that they could have Bermuda grass in the infield and outfield. A castor-bean home run fence was grown, which reached eight to ten feet in height.

After the field was laid out, the next project was a grandstand. "We needed lumber," said Harvey Zenimura. "We were in Block 28, and the lumberyard was way across the other side of the camp, probably another mile away. We'd go out there in the middle of the night and get lumber and lug it all the way out into the sagebrush, bury it in the desert and then go back later and get it as we needed it. The camp officials probably knew what was going on, but nobody said anything."

When the stands were completed, the bleachers had four or five rows. Zenimura went so far as to provide individual box seats on the planks. "My

In 1942, the Gila River Eagles baseball team defeated the three-time defending state championship team from Tucson High School. With the score tied at ten in the tenth inning, Harvey Zenimura drove a bases-loaded, game-winning single through the infield, providing a morale-lifting victory for thousands of fans who attended the game. *Courtesy Tets Furukawa.*

dad marked the benches with paint," remarked Harvey. He drew lines and put numbers in so that anybody who donated a lot of money would get his good box seat." The park's "box office" consisted of coffee cans at two different entrances where fans could deposit donations to watch the game. In addition, a collection was taken up at every game. Zenimura used the proceeds to have baseball equipment shipped from a Fresno sporting goods dealer. In a 1962 interview, he claimed to have ordered about $2,000 worth of equipment from Holman's Sporting Goods.

Actor Noriyuki "Pat" Morita, who was interned with his family at Gila River and grew up to star in *The Karate Kid* and other movies, retained a vivid memory of the work that went into maintaining the diamond: "I remember watching this little old brown guy watering down the infield with this huge hose. He used to have his kids dragging the infield and throwing out all the rocks. Jeez, I was glad I wasn't them. They worked like mules." Keeping the field in playing condition, and ensuring that fans were as comfortable as possible, demanded constant labor. Cement-drying pads covered the dugouts and bleachers to provide shade against the desert sun, while the pebbles strained from the infield were spread below the bleachers and on the dugout floors to keep the dust down.

Thirty-two teams in three divisions competed at Gila River, where the climate allowed for practically year-round play. "The games were very competitive," recalled James Tomooka. As in the other camps, playing, watching and supporting baseball brought a sense of normalcy to very abnormal lives and created a social and positive atmosphere. As Pat Morita described it, "The teenagers and adults would gather every night to watch the games. I'd never seen a live baseball game before, so this was my introduction to baseball— sitting and cheering with a couple thousand rabid fans." For Pat and other fans, recalling better times and longing for their return, Kenichi Zenimura's diamond in the sagebrush was truly a field of dreams.

TRIUMPH AND TRAGEDY AT TULE LAKE

California's Tule Lake detention facility was primarily for hardcore internees and radicals who wanted to repatriate to Japan or who gave the "wrong" answers on a government questionnaire that was vague and could be misinterpreted. Some of these residents felt that if America was going to imprison them just because of their race, they wanted out.

Almost nineteen thousand internees filled the Tule Lake compound. They were divided into two main factions, one pro-Japan and the other loyal to the United States. This split in loyalty made for a highly volatile situation. Leading the pro-Japan block were Kibei—American-born Nisei who had been educated in Japan and were not only strong partisans of the Rising Sun but also particularly rabid baseball fans.

The camp attracted considerable notice from the outside world. On May 2, 1944, under the headline "All of Tule Lake Turns Out for Baseball Season," the *San Francisco Chronicle* reported, "Baseball season opened at Tule Lake Internment Camp on the heels of ceremonies celebrating the birthday of the Emperor of Japan over the weekend, the War Relocation Authority announced yesterday. Ceremonies Saturday were brief and the day passed without incident, according to the War Relocation Authority (WRA). The Tule Lake Baseball Convention was opened by project director Ray Best, who threw out the first ball for the opening game. More than half of the 18,000 residents of the center were present for the game, it was announced." There were fifteen "major-league" and twenty-three "minor-league" teams for the 1944 season. On this day, the Manzanar team played the Poston squad. Manzanar and Poston players traveled to Tule Lake for the express purpose of the baseball tournament. At Tule Lake, there would be fans from their own regions or those who had transferred from another camp. As usual for any

千九百四十五年
於鶴嶺湖大壽野球部記念寫真

The 1945 Taisei team from Tule Lake, California, featured player-coach Ed Tsukimura (bottom row, far left), an all-star outfielder who competed against many Pacific Coast League and Hall of Fame legends in his career. *Ed Tsukimura collection.*

Safe at home. A Manzanar catcher takes a throw at home in a game at the Tule Lake, California detention camp. *Courtesy Masao Iriyama.*

Thousands of fans cheer at a game at Tule Lake, California. *Courtesy Masao Iriyama.*

game involving the Manzanar team, there was a better than average turnout. "Our fans had an organized rooting section led by Kibei," said Barry Tamura, a member of the Manzanar team. "They had the flags just like you see in Japanese stadiums today. We sure drew the crowds. They all wanted to see our cheerleading team." This included a prominent group of burly fishermen from the harbor community of San Pedro who had a well-deserved reputation for being hotheaded and always ready to mix things up.

A 1944 game between Manzanar and Poston proved to be one of the classic contests played on the Tule Lake grounds, one that illustrates the passionate fandom of the camp's internees. After nine innings, the score was tied 5–5. In the top of the fourteenth, Poston broke through against Manzanar pitcher Jim Tamura for three runs. In the Manzanar half, with a runner on second and two out, shortstop George Tamura, the younger brother of Jim and Barry, got a hit, advancing the runner to third. The next batter belted a fly into the gap in left field. Hugo Nishimoto was umpiring at first base. "The left fielder went up and jumped," he related, "and the ball was deflected off his glove, but the center fielder who was backing him up caught it. Ed Tanaka, the third base umpire, and I both raised our hands [to signal] out. Oh boy! The Manzanar fans couldn't take it, and they started storming out onto the field." The Manzanar rooters complained vociferously that the ball had been trapped. George Tamura described the ensuing mêlée:

This fellow who was a real close friend of ours went after the Poston team himself, right in their dugout. George Miyakawa got hit over the head with a chair and was bleeding. I saw his dad go in there pulling him out with a bloody head. That really started it all. All these big boozers came out of the sands with fire in their eyes, and we were in the infield and we held everybody back. In the pandemonium, the umpires and Poston center fielder had to be escorted back to their blocks. After things settled down a bit, the player who claimed he caught the ball came to our block with his father and mother and apologized to our friends and family. After that, he quit baseball. Later on, we asked our friend why he went into the dugout like that, and he told us he felt sorry for Jim. Jim was pitching such a good game, and we hated to see him get robbed of a win.

Of course, not all games resulted in such wild displays. On a less intense side, the four Tomooka brothers led the Guadalupe team that had been transferred basically intact from Gila River to the Tule Lake facility. They recruited more players to their team and ended up winning the Taiseiyo Pacific Division championship. They later went on to take three straight from the Tule Lake Nippon, winners of the Taiyo Atlantic Division title, for the overall camp crown.

Ryo Kashiwagi of the Tule Lake Wakabas remembers playing the champions, Guadalupe YMBA:

Everyone in camp was there. We didn't have an outfield fence, but the people watching lined the entire outfield to make a fence. I was considered the home run hitter of the team. When I stepped up there and connected, I hit this towering deep drive into left field. Everyone thought it was a home run, but little did I realize that Guadalupe's left fielder, Masayoshi "Massy" Tomooka, fast as a jackrabbit, took off after the ball and cut his way through the left-field human wall of the crowd and kept running. Back, back, back. I was into my home run trot around third base and was shocked when a roar came up from the crowd. Massy Tomooka had outrun the ball in the middle of all these people and caught it with his back to home plate. This was like Willie Mays robbing Vic Wertz, except Massy ran through a wall of people to make the catch of the day. I'll never forget it. I was robbed.

Kaz "Mr. Baseball" Ikeda of the Arroyo Grande YMBA team was also well acquainted with Tomooka's skill. "Massy's been robbing

The 1944 Guadalupe Nisei championship team gathers for a team picture at Tule Lake, California. *Courtesy James Tomooka.*

This 1944 panoramic view of the Tule Lake Stadium, with its multiple guard towers, is more reminiscent of *Stalag 17* in Germany than it is of an American baseball park. However, it is also representative of Americans keeping the American pastime alive, even from behind barbed-wire fences. *Courtesy Masao Iriyama.*

This Gila River Eagles team took a road trip to the Heart Mountain, Wyoming detention camp. It's ironic to think of a group of "enemy aliens" putting on uniforms and traveling to distant locations to play baseball, especially since most of the baseball parks were built on the outside of the barbed wire. *Courtesy of Hisa Iwamoto.*

people his entire life," said the ballplayer, who himself had huge hits taken away by Massy.

Even today, memories of individual plays and exciting games in the internment camps linger, but they can never obscure the harsh reality that these contests were taking place under conditions of imprisonment. Other memories persist as well, such as the remembrance of Shoichi James Okamoto. On May 2, 1944, Okamoto was shot to death by a guard at Tule Lake after stopping a construction truck at the main gate for permission to pass. The guard, Private Bernard Goe, would be acquitted after being fined one dollar for "unauthorized use of government property—a bullet."

IRONIES OF WAR

One of the ironies of baseball behind barbed wire was that Japanese Americans were considered enemy aliens and were confined to detention camps, but if they put on baseball uniforms, they were given free passage

Slinging southpaws at the University of Connecticut in 1945 included Ernie Korvo, Kay Kiyokawa and Bob Hill. Kiyokawa was also the starting running back on the University of Connecticut football team. Kiyokawa was among more than five hundred Nisei students who attended college under the sponsorship of the Quaker Church. *Courtesy Kay Kiyokawa.*

to take road trips. Teams from Gila River, for example, traveled to Heart Mountain, Wyoming, and Amache, Colorado, to play baseball. "The ballplayers would usually travel in small groups of five or six so that we would not create attention," said Howard Zenimura. "None of the citizens of the different towns and cities we passed through paid us much attention." The temporarily liberated internees would travel by Greyhound bus hundreds of miles for a one- or two-week road trip.

Another irony was that most of the camps' baseball diamonds were actually built on the outside of the barbed-wire enclosures. Sab Yamada recalled, "Where would you run to? There were hundreds of miles of desert, and most of the government officials were upset that they were in the desert, too. There was no treachery or espionage going on in the camps."

If interned ballplayers could leave the camps, sometimes players from the outside world could come in. One of the biggest upsets in Arizona baseball history took place on Gila River's Zenimura Field. A three-time state championship team from a high school in Tucson came into the detention center to play the Gila River Eagles. For the young Tucson players, it must have felt eerie to enter a camp with barbed wire and guard towers to play a high school team in baseball. Camp director Bennett scoffed at the idea that a three-time state championship team would come in to play a camp team that was undefeated against teams like Mesa, Tollison and Canal Camp but that could in no way match the size and depth of the Tucson squad. Despite Bennett's skepticism, however, the game went into extra innings with the score tied 10–10. In the tenth inning, Harvey Zenimura came to the plate with the bases loaded. The Tucson pitcher's first three pitches were outside the strike zone, and Harvey did not swing. The next two pitches were strikes, and Harvey had yet to swing the bat. Now the count was full, and the game was on the line. On the sixth pitch, Harvey swung and ripped a line drive between third base and shortstop for the game-winning hit.

Thousands of internees were watching this game, and for them it was much more than just a baseball victory. It was a moral victory that represented coming from behind against all odds. To this day, the Eagles' triumph is still celebrated for its high achievements and its boost to Japanese Americans' self-esteem. George Kataoka, a member of the winning team, said, "You know, the Tucson paper said that it was a bloop single that won the game for them. Heck, that was no bloop single. Kenshi [Harvey] ripped that ball right between third and shortstop." Prior to this interview, George had said that he didn't remember anything about any of the camp history or any of the baseball games because it had been almost sixty years ago. For many of the Nisei generation, the memories that return are the positive ones, while the negative experiences of camp life are buried and put to rest. That, too, is one of the ironies of this wartime tragedy.

Perhaps the greatest irony of all was that men could create a measure of fun and pleasure in such bleak circumstances. Recognized poet Lawson Inada, who was detained in camps in Arkansas and Colorado, wrote the following poem, "A Boy Among Men," for Fred Yoshikawa and Kenichi Zenimura:

> *Don't be deceived*
> *By the smiles.*
> *These are tough,*
> *Strong men*
> *Wise to the ways*
> *Of strategies*
> *And survival.*

Don't be deceived
By the smiles.
These are the men
Who could handle
Crates and shovels,
Who could handle
Heat.

Don't be deceived
By the smiles.
These are the men
Who could shoulder
History,
Who could shoulder
Responsibility.

Don't be deceived
By the smiles.
These are the men
Of serious
Spirit,
Of serious
Dignity.

Don't be deceived
By the smiles.
These are the men
Who could give
And take
As good as any,
On a level field.

Don't be deceived
By the smiles.
These are the men
Of grace
And skill,
Of power
And will,

Who could stride
From the shadows
Of barracks
And guard towers
Just to play
A little ball—
Smiling!

American Society of Friends Sponsorship

The grave injustice of internment did not go unrecognized by all Americans. One group in particular tried to ameliorate the fate of Japanese Americans who had been stripped of property, freedom and opportunity. During the war, members of the Quaker religion reached out to the people interned in the detention camps, seeking students to sponsor for college educations.

Kay Kiyokawa was one of the star pitchers for the Hood River Nisei. While he was at Tule Lake, a group of Quakers from Connecticut entered the camp seeking to sponsor Nisei who were qualified in terms of age and desired to go to college. The only catch was that the sponsored students would have to relocate to Ohio State, the University of Connecticut or the University of Delaware.

Over five hundred Nisei men and women took advantage of the Quakers' generosity and compassion. Among them was Kay Kiyokawa, who said goodbye to his parents and left the camp to attend college. During his prewar playing days, Kay had been a starting pitcher for the Oregon State Beavers. Now he became not only a starting pitcher for the University of Connecticut baseball team but also an all-conference running back for the football team. Kay was only four feet, ten inches tall, but he never let his size restrict his goals. "I always had a desire to play baseball," he said, "and my size was never an issue. When I started playing football at a college level, I knew I had to be physically and mentally strong." Kiyokawa remembers playing an away game against the University of Maine. "The first time I went up to bat, some people in the stands were chanting, 'Hey Tojo.'" Tojo was the general of the Empire of Japan who led his country into war against the United States. Kiyokawa promptly lined a double down the left-field line. The catcalls continued—"Tojo, Tojo"—during his second at-bat. This time, he drove a triple into the outfield gap between left and center. The third time up, the only yells he heard were, "Slugger, Slugger." In only three plate appearances, Kay was able to break down negative feelings and turn them into positive perceptions.

Nisei Soldiers-Ballplayers

A further irony of World War II was that a number of Japanese Americans fought with distinction for the same country that had put the vast majority of their people behind barbed wire. The 100th Infantry Battalion was a U.S. Army battalion made up of Nisei from Hawaii that saw heavy action in Italy, France and Germany. The 442nd Mainland Nisei, the 100th Hawaiian Nisei and the MIS (Military Intelligence Service), which was made up of Nisei soldiers, were among the most decorated units in services for their size.

Like their brethren in the camps, Nisei soldiers showed their prowess on the diamond as well as on the battlefield. One soldier, Joe Takata, was a legendary player in the Hawaiian Islands before the war. After enlisting in Hawaii, he was sent to the mainland and stationed at Camp Robinson, Arkansas, for basic training. He ended up playing for the 100th team. In June 1943, while training in Camp Shelby, Mississippi, the squad journeyed to the Jerome detention camp to play a team of Nisei interns predominantly made up of members of the Florin Athletic Club. Joe became a favorite of the fans in Jerome.

The battalion team went on to play a memorable contest in North Africa. Ted Hirayama, the team's coach, recalled, "From Arkansas, we were supposed to head to Europe to begin our battle in Italy. But Milton Eisenhower [head of the War Relocation Authority] had heard that we had this great baseball team, so General Ryder requested that our Nisei team go to North Africa first to play the 168th Infantry Regiment of the 34th Division team, which was one of their powerhouse baseball clubs. So before we got ready to do combat in Italy, we played this last game. It was a close game all the way to the ninth inning, and they had been pitching away from Joe Takata and his power, either walking him or setting him up with breaking balls. Because we got into the late innings, they had to replace their starter with a relief pitcher." Joe Takata settled into the batter's box and set himself. The pitcher rocked and tried to throw a fastball by him. Crack! Joe smacked

The legendary 100th Battalion baseball team played its last game at a North African army base. In his last at-bat, Joe Takata (second row, far right) hit a long game-winning home run. The next road trip for the 100th was to Italy, where Takata was the first member of the battalion to be killed in action. *Courtesy Japanese American National Museum.*

the ball over the fence! This would be his last home run—and also his last at-bat. Shortly after arriving in Italy and heroically taking out two pillboxes single-handedly, Joe was hit with flying shrapnel and killed. He became the first member of the 100th Battalion to be killed in action. The legendary Ted Williams, in his last major-league at-bat, ended his career with a home run. In a sense, Joe Takata's story paralleled that of Williams—only in Joe's case, the ending was truly final.

Another Nisei soldier saw the course of his baseball career changed by the war. John Murakami grew up in Sherwood, Oregon. At sixteen, he played organized baseball for the first time with a team from the Buddhist Temple. The next year, he caught on with the Portland Mikados. He practically lived at the Vaughn Street Ball Park. He was a center fielder with good range and a strong arm. In 1942, John's parents were shipped off to the Minidoka internment camp in the badlands of Idaho. John joined the army as a member of the 442nd Regimental Combat Team. He was wounded in Italy and came home with a useless right arm, so he learned to throw left-handed and took up the game again with the Oregon Nisei vets.

In 1945, a group of Nisei soldiers in the Military Intelligence Service (MIS) had the chance to play against New York Yankee pitcher Spurgeon "Spud" Chandler. Chandler, whose lifetime winning percentage in the major leagues was a lofty .717, won a league-leading twenty games that year and would add two more victories in the World Series. That September, his wife was hospitalized at the Mayo Clinic in Rochester, Minnesota. To stay sharp, Chandler asked to pitch for the home team against the all-Nisei Fort Snelling MIS all-star team, which included brothers Jim, Yosh and Bill Tsukamoto. The three brothers had been released from the Jerome, Arkansas detention facility after volunteering for the MIS while their parents remained confined.

Chandler's team and the Nisei squad squared off for a double-header. In the sixth inning of the first game, Bill Tsukamoto came up with a man on base and faced the hard-throwing Yankee ace. Bill recalled, "He tried to throw a curve ball, and it hung over the plate belt-high. I waited on it and drove it to left field down the line." Sadly for Bill, the crowd overflowed onto the playing field, and a spectator grabbed the ball, holding him to a triple on what ordinarily would have been a home run. The hit was still good enough to beat Chandler's team 4–2, and the Nisei went on to win the second game as well to sweep the twin bill.

THE LEGACY OF THE CAMPS

The story of desert diamonds behind barbed wire demonstrates that an understanding of history can overcome the fear and misunderstanding that awaken intolerance. The arts and sports practiced by the internees were not entertainment but rather approaches for finding, articulating and preserving meaning in a senseless situation. As former internee Pete Mitsui, founder of the San Fernando Aces said, "The ball club was an important part of the community identity. Examining that history today is a way to explain not only what happened but why the internment camp episode occurred, as well as how the 1942 events connect to today's issues."

Japanese Americans' connection to the love of the game is in part a search for identity as Americans in a new land and culture that are constantly in flux. Baseball is a nexus where different cultures intersect and a touchstone for comparing and contrasting the experiences of diverse groups in America. Because Japanese Americans relied on baseball to help them cope during the years of anguish at the internment camps, baseball also serves as a lens through which to view camp history. This baseball lens can provide an opportunity for people to discuss the delicate and troublesome stories of internment because baseball provides the common element with which people of diverse cultures can identify.

For Japanese Americans interned during World War II, playing, watching and supporting baseball inside America's concentration camps brought a sense of normalcy to very abnormal lives. *Toyo Miyatake collection.*

American citizens who were of the Issei and Nisei generations were imprisoned by their own government primarily because they looked like the enemy, whereas German and Italian Americans did not. As a result, the internment camp experience is central to a great deal of Japanese American culture. Historian Rosalyn Tonai notes, "The history of Japanese American baseball is a paradoxical story of inclusion and assimilation within a larger context of exclusion from the majority culture. Against the backdrop of segregation, discrimination, and exclusionary laws, baseball was passionately played within the community by local teams beginning with the very first Issei immigrants."

By the time of the internment camps, baseball was firmly entrenched in Japanese American culture. At the start of the internment, conditions in the assembly centers and camps were dismal, and morale was low. It was natural for the internees to turn to baseball as a way to bring a sense of normalcy to daily life. Playing and watching baseball created a positive social atmosphere, encouraged physical conditioning and maintained self-esteem despite the harsh conditions of incarceration in remote and desolate camps. Ironically, America's national game helped to sustain the people singled out as "enemy aliens." The task of creating and maintaining diamonds like Zenimura Field linked the internees to their prewar life, their culture and to one another.

Today, Zenimura Field no longer exists. Near its old location, an olive orchard grows in the desert. In the 1990s, Pat Morita made a pilgrimage to the Gila River site. "Kenichi Zenimura showed that with effort and persistence, you can overcome the harshness of adversity," said Morita. "Zenimura and others created a fraternal community in the desert—and baseball was a glue."

Baseball continued to play a role in bringing the community back together after the war. After 1945, most Japanese Americans had very little. Most had lost everything, but they could still meet every Sunday on the ball field, forging community and identity. In this way, baseball helped nurse the deep wounds of the war. Perhaps today the story of baseball behind barbed wire can help to transform American communities throughout the nation with its example of heroic triumph over discrimination.

There is a story that perhaps symbolizes both the pain and the healing that can come from the memory of the Japanese American experience during the war. It involves Norman Mineta, a former congressman and mayor of San Jose. "I'll never forget walking into the detention facility in my Cub Scout uniform and with my prize possession, my baseball bat and glove," Mineta recalled years later. "The guard at the gate stopped me and took my bat away from me, saying it was a weapon. This was my most prized possession, and he took it away." Later, Mineta, as a U.S. congressman, had a second traumatic experience involving a baseball bat. One fan, having heard the story of this Mineta's childhood experience, presented him with a baseball bat signed by two of his heros, Henry Aaron and Sahaharu Oh, the all-time home run kings of the United States and Japan, respectively. After expressing his appreciation and gratitude, Mineta took the bat back to his office. A few minutes later, there was a knock at the door. One of the congressman's aides reminded him that the bat was a gift worth more than $250, and to accept it would have been illegal. So for the second time in Norman Mineta's life, he had to surrender his most prized possession, a baseball bat, to the government.

Fortunately, the story has a happy ending. When Mineta retired from congress, the same fan again presented him with the autographed bat. Now that he was a private citizen, there were no laws to prevent him from accepting both the honor and the gift. This time former Cub Scout, internee and distinguished public servant Norman Mineta would get to keep his cherished bat.

Chapter 7

POSTWAR BASEBALL IN AMERICA AND JAPAN: RESETTLEMENT, REORGANIZATION AND RECONCILIATION

Try to speed up the mutual feeling between the Americans and the Japanese Americans. It is much easier to make efforts of starting a better understanding between us in the field of sports than trying to talk your way through the rough spots.
—*Kenichi Zenimura*

After January 1945, Americans confined behind barbed wire were allowed to leave. The WRA referred to the movement of Japanese Americans out of restricted areas and internment camps as voluntary "resettlement." Approximately 120,000 Japanese Americans passed the various security clearances and resumed their lives, many of them in new and unfamiliar surroundings.

The WRA believed that it was important for Japanese Americans not to go back to the West Coast and to the tightknit communities and Japan towns from which they had come. Agency officials felt that the Nisei and Issei should expand their horizons by going to different parts of the country, becoming more "Americanized" and blending in with the local population. There was a chance of greater economic opportunity and less discrimination in eastern and midwestern cities, where few people had seen Japanese Americans before, and the former internees might be able to ease labor shortages in these areas brought on by the war.

Every former internee had to start over again from the beginning. "When we got out of the camp," recalled Masao Hirata, "they gave us only twenty-five dollars per person. I experienced unspeakable hardship to support all

Where have you gone Joe DiMaggio? In this case, "Joltin' Joe" had gone to a 1954 batting clinic for the Hiroshima Carp baseball team of the Japanese Central League. American-born Harvey Zenimura (front row, fourth from left) and son of Kenichi takes note. The clinic must have been successful because Zenimura went on to become a two-time all-star. *Courtesy Cappy Harada.*

my family. I will never forget it." Hirata and his family had no place to stay, no car and no tools to cut the tall weeds that had taken over his farm. "But I had to work to support my family, so I borrowed old tools and worked on my farm." Approximately 90 percent of Japanese Americans who had land, houses and property before the war lost everything. One Issei farmer testified shortly after his return to California:

> *Before the war, I had twenty acres in Berryessa. Good land, two good homes, very nice farm. During the war, hysteria—everybody said sell, sell, sell. Maybe lose it all. A lawyer wrote to me and said sell. I sell for $650 an acre. Now the same land is $1,500 an acre. I lose, and I cannot help. All gone. Now I live in hostile work-like land. Pick cherries, pick pears, pick apricots, pick tomatoes—just like when first come. Pretty soon—maybe one*

year, maybe two years—find place. Pretty hard now. No use look back. Go crazy think about all lost. Have to start all over again like when come from Japan, but faster this time.

After the war ended, most Nisei and Issei felt that they were innocent victims of racism and wartime hysteria. Not a single case of espionage or sabotage had ever been attributed to Japanese Americans. They had been singled out, uprooted from their homes and exiled into internment camps under the false premise of military necessity. It was indeed amazing that under those circumstances, there were Nisei men and women who volunteered for service in the armed forces to prove their loyalty to the United States. They distinguished themselves with uncommon valor. After the war, they too returned to the larger society. The long ordeal of confinement was over, but the task of rebuilding was only beginning. In the postwar period of economic opportunities, Nisei were able to make great strides in fields such as civil service, education, law—and baseball.

Rebuilding American Teams

"Even after the war, we were considered terrible, traitors," Henry Honda remembered. "Baseball was a way to prove ourselves loyal." After struggling to contain his feelings, Honda succumbed. "You know they stuck us in a goddamn internment camp—hell, concentration camp. Then they take you out after two years and give you a rifle." His hands shook as tears fell. "This is America?"

Honda, a fire-balling pitcher for of the San Jose Asahi, had been signed by the Cleveland Indians in 1941. He was on the verge of being called up to the majors when bombs fell on Pearl Harbor. Honda's contract was yanked, and his good years were squandered in the Manzanar internment camp in California. Later, Honda said, "You know, I loved baseball then, in the prewar years, and I had a pretty good chance to have a career. I still pitched in the camps and had a pretty good baseball season and career inside the camps, but when I got out, my career hopes ended." He added tearfully, "I loved baseball then, and I still love baseball now."

Baseball had been a way of life for many Japanese Americans before the war and had provided a catharsis during internment. Now the challenge was

In Hood River, Oregon, trees formed the backdrop (and sometimes the backstop) for Nisei ballplayers such as John Murakami. Oregon and Washington State were hotbeds of Nisei baseball in the Pacific Northwest. *Courtesy John Murakami.*

to regroup, resettle and keep the torch burning for baseball in the postwar period. Once again, Japanese Americans sought to claim a space in America where they could compete on a level playing field. Baseball could help to level the field.

Kenichi Zenimura expressed this idea in his last article for the camp newspaper as baseball coach at Gila River. Zenimura began with a heartfelt tip of his cap to the players and their supporters in the camp:

May I take this opportunity to thank each and every one for their fine cooperation shown me during the past three years here at Gila River. Also, I appreciate the untiring efforts shown by all members of various clubs and organizations in making the baseball league a successful one. I am about to leave the center soon, and before I do, I wish to extend my deepest appreciation to all the players on the Gila "All-Star" team, who have an unblemished record for the last three seasons against outside competition. The fine men's conduct, great showmanship, and their ever-ready heads-up baseball illustrated on the diamond makes me very proud. Their fine sportsmanship on and off the field. It was through your efforts that such a record can be boasted. Also, many of the outside teams that have played us have praised the Gila boys. By playing a clean and fast game, they wish that they had some of the boys on their team. For this I am very glad of the boys who have played under my guidance and those who have been playing on other teams on the league...Through the help of all the players, Gila can be proud of boasting to have the finest diamond in all the centers to play and practice on.

To you fans, I wish to express my thanks for your generous support and cooperation in making the league a success...The boys and I really appreciated what you have done for us. Though I am on the outside, I'll always remember the swell time I had playing baseball here in Gila. I will also be thinking of you players and fans. My memories will always be here at Gila.

Then the farsighted coach turned his attention to the future:

Sooner or later everyone will have to relocate, and when we do please remember that you are as good as the other fellows—so don't be backward, show them what you can do. Those who have played under my guidance, on my team, or on the all-star teams, I have all the confidence in the world of your making the grade on any high school or college, and if given the chance, don't let them come and ask you but go out there on your own accord and let yourself be seen. This is one of the easiest ways of making friends.

I will be returning to Fresno and while I am there will try to make a team to play in the league in the city. Try to speed up the mutual feeling between the Americans and the Japanese Americans. It is much easier to make efforts of starting a better understanding between us in the field of sports than trying to talk your way through the rough spots. So if any of you fellows ever drop down in Fresno way, drop in and see me. We can talk over old times. So till then, again, may I wish all of you the best of luck and success.

Sincerely yours,
Kenny Zenimura

Postwar resettlement brought a new era of reorganization and recommitment in baseball and in the larger community. Since Japanese Americans were encouraged to resettle in areas away from the Pacific Coast, many had to move to the East and Midwest to start over again. Akiko Mitsui said, "When we were leaving on the trains [for the camps], we saw signs from many of the people saying, 'Get out and don't come back' or 'You're never coming back to California.' So once we were in the camps, we never thought we would return." Eventually, most Japanese Americans did return to the West, but many communities never regained their prewar vibrancy.

In baseball, teams from Northern, Southern and Central California once again took up the quest for bragging rights for their regions and communities. But Japanese American baseball in the postwar period could not recover all the spirit and vitality of the prewar era. Many of the Issei who had been so supportive of the efforts of Nisei ballplayers were shells of their former selves, severely diminished in health and energy, while younger generations found interest in other sports. Moreover, as Japanese Americans acculturated into society, Nisei baseball mirrored the fate of the Negro Leagues and started to fade into the background. Ironically, the internment period contributed to this result by developing an even better quality of ballplayers. With little else to do but practice and play every day—particularly in the Arizona desert, where baseball could be played practically year-round—many fine Nisei ballplayers honed their skills while in the camps. Howard Zenimura said, "I mean, we played baseball year-round. We would play early in the morning, take a break in the afternoon because of the searing heat and the sun being so hot and then come back and play in the late afternoon again. That's why many of us, once we got out of camp, were able to make college teams rather easily—because our skill level was so high."

After the war, well-organized baseball leagues made up of these players sprang up wherever former internees resettled, and baseball once again gave Japanese Americans a meaningful recreational outlet. At the same time, a new wave of college-level athletes began to appear, raising the bar of excellence in the newly formed communities of Nikkei (all-Japanese American generations). Increasingly, however, the Nisei began to assimilate into mainstream society as other Americans came to realize the hardships and sacrifice suffered by Japanese Americans during their time of exile.

Still, the battle against prejudice was far from won. Once again, baseball helped Japanese Americans cross the racial divide. In Sanger, California, seven out of the nine starters on the 1947 high school valley championship team were Nisei. Dan Takeuchi remembers, "I remember when we came back from camp and established ourselves with our baseball team in high school. Our coach, Huntley Dayton, really believed that through baseball we were going to be able to combat a lot of discrimination and bitterness that many other people felt, and we took our shots and ribbing at most of the games. They would taunt us with racial slurs while we were playing, but our coach and teammates backed us up and we were able to really do a lot of healing—not only for ourselves, but to let others know that we were just going to go on very positively."

PRISON BASEBALL

A fascinating sidelight in the history of Japanese American baseball both before and after the war concerns games played against prison inmates.

One such prewar contest took place in Washington State, where the serene backdrop of rolling hills and green pastures suddenly gives way to the mammoth cold cement walls of Walla Walla State Penitentiary. One day in 1938, a group of men gathered in front of the gates, waiting to enter the notorious prison. The steel doors opened, and the squad of Wapato Nippon entered the compound. "It really makes you appreciate freedom when the doors shut on you," observed Harry Honda, the leader of the Wapato team. Harry and his teammates had been invited into the prison by the Walla Walla baseball team. The Nippon had built a reputation for baseball excellence that had even carried over the walls of the institution.

Whistles sounded, and like clockwork a very quiet and orchestrated flow of women filed into the back rows of the stadium. Then the male prisoners entered, accompanied by shotgun-toting guards. A thunderous roar rose from the stands when the Walla Walla team appeared. Despite the strangeness of the surroundings, the cheering of the fans helped to settle the Nippon into game mode, and the contest began.

The 1952 Lodi Athletic Club challenged the Grey Eagles of Folsom Prison at the prison. Because of a short right-field wall, all of the prisoners in the game chose to bat left-handed. The Grey Eagles won the contest, but all in the packed crowd left the field halfway through the game. It seems that the exercise period was over. *Courtesy Mas Okuhara.*

"I remember the name of the pitcher was 'Chink' Johnson," Harry Honda related. "They said he was an ex-pro player that fell on hard times. I wonder if that was his real name, or if they wanted to see if his name would rattle us." Although the Grey Eagles won, the Wapato team performed well in the hard-fought game, which gave the inmates a chance to forget their confinement for a few hours. Three years later, the Wapato team would again play in conditions of confinement, this time as the resident home team of the Heart Mountain, Wyoming detention camp.

After the war, another prominent Japanese American team, the Lodi Athletic Club, traveled to Folsom State Penitentiary in California to play an exhibition game with the prisoners. Legendary manager Mas Okuhara described the experience:

When we went inside the prison, there were hundreds and hundreds of fans in the stands, and the team was called the Folsom Gray Eagles. What was amazing was that every batter batted left-handed, and after a few home runs over the short right-field fence, we understood why. This Gray Eagle team took advantage of that short right-field wall and continued to hit home run after home run after home run. During the middle of the game, all of a sudden the fans in the stands emptied. Then we realized that their exercise period had ended, so all the fans had to leave. The Folsom Eagles eventually won the game. As far as the Lodi team, they were glad and relieved to be the visitors in this contest.

HEALING THE WOUNDS OF WAR

Across the Pacific, Japan faced the enormous challenge of rebuilding a war-torn country under conditions of apocalyptic devastation. Cities and townships had crumbled, and the spirits of the Japanese were at an all-time low. The entire country was submerged in a deep depression, both financially and emotionally. Reaction to the postwar occupation by American troops at times became very bitter and hostile. Lack of provisions amid the carnage of the villages and neighborhoods made tensions run very high, and protests were commonplace.

General MacArthur turned to his staff for recommendations to quell the rioting and defuse the animosity toward the troops. Lieutenant Cappy Harada, a Nisei, stood before his peers and suggested American baseball tours of goodwill. MacArthur responded, "What are we waiting for?" He then passed the word that every accommodation possible was to be made to revive baseball in Japan. Not only did he want to give the game back to the people of Japan, but he also recognized baseball as an invaluable instrument for helping to build Japan into a new democratic nation.

O'Doul's San Francisco Seals of the Pacific Coast League arrived in Japan in 1949 to open a ten-game series, three against American service teams and seven against Japanese clubs. This was O'Doul's third appearance in Japan. He had been to Japan in 1931 and 1934, and in all his subsequent trips, Lefty took particular pains to be nice to the children. On the road to his quarters after landing at Haneda Airport in 1949, O'Doul was struck by the sad faces of the kids who were silently lined up to greet him.

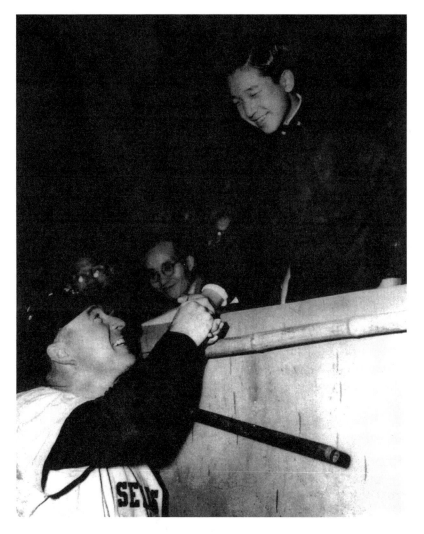

Young Prince Akihito, currently emperor of Japan, exchanges handshakes and "banzais" with Lefty O'Doul of the San Francisco Seals, 1949. O'Doul helped name Japan's first prewar pro team the Tokyo Giants. *Courtesy Cappy Harada.*

"Banzai!" O'Doul called while waving his arms. There was no response from the children. "What's the matter?" Lefty asked Lieutenant Cappy Harada, who was acting as his interpreter. "The land is now occupied, Lefty," the lieutenant replied. "No banzai." Back in 1931 and 1934, it was the youngsters who were doing most of the "banzai" (bravo) in greetings to Lefty and the American all-stars.

At a press conference shortly after his arrival, O'Doul said, "I have more friends in Japan than I have in America." Rich Dempsey, a pitcher with the Seals on the tour, remembers that the Japanese responded to O'Doul "almost like he was a biblical character." Dempsey went on, "I have seldom seen so much adoration. He was idolized." During Lefty's earlier visits, the Japanese people sensed that he liked their country. He enjoyed the food, made efforts to learn the language and helped the ballplayers with their batting and other baseball skills. Sincerity needs no translation, and Lefty's authenticity had universal appeal for the Japanese people, especially the children.

The Seals ten-game series drew over 500,000 fans. Even a pair of contests played during a rainstorm in Nagoya drew over 140,000. As a result of the tour, more than $100,000 went to Japanese charities.

O'Doul was quoted as saying, "When I was here years ago, their cry was always 'banzai, banzai.' But they were so depressed when I arrived here [this time]. When I hollered 'banzai' to them, they didn't even respond." But by the time Lefty left for home six weeks later, he said, "All of Japan was 'banzaiing' again." In a little over a month, O'Doul and the San Francisco Seals had managed to restore much of the nation's morale. They broke the postwar tension in Japanese-American relations and created a bridge for friendship between the countries.

"All the diplomats together would not have been able to do that," MacArthur said later. "This is the greatest piece of diplomacy ever." General Matthew B. Ridgeway, who succeeded MacArthur as the supreme commander of Allied forces in Japan in 1951, said, "Words cannot describe Lefty's wonderful contributions to baseball and to the postwar rebuilding effort." Matsutaro Shoriki, past owner and president of the Yomiuri Giants, reflected deep feelings of the American generals when he said, "The tour was the most successful goodwill event ever made on an international scale at the time." Even Emperor Hirohito was so appreciative that he summoned San Francisco Seals president Paul Fagin and vice-president Charlie Graham to the Imperial Palace to thank them personally for all they had done. Much of the credit for the success of the Seals' tour belongs to Lieutenant Cappy Harada, who was appointed by General MacArthur to head the joint committee of the U.S./Japan Goodwill Baseball Tour. Harada led the effort to rehabilitate sports in Japan in the postwar years and fought many hours with officers of the U.S. forces to preserve athletic facilities for the people of Japan. He assisted in reconstructing professional baseball and succeeded in getting the Allied forces' motor pool moved out of Korakuen Stadium, which no longer exists. He was responsible for making night baseball in Japan

During a rainy Japanese baseball game in Tokyo, American baseball hero Lefty O'Doul received unqualified fan support and an umbrella. *Courtesy San Francisco Library.*

The Yomiuri Giants meet Lefty O'Doul. O'Doul's 1949 ten-game series in Japan drew over 500,000 fans. *Courtesy San Francisco Library.*

possible by securing from MacArthur's headquarters a permit for Korakuen Stadium to procure vital electric cable so that lights could be installed for Japanese professional baseball.

Cappy Harada grew up in Santa Maria, California, and earned his nickname by being high school captain of the football, baseball and basketball squads. An infielder, Cappy was to have reported to the Cardinals for spring training in 1942, but the day after Pearl Harbor, he enlisted in the army. "Some people thought I must have taken off to become a spy," Cappy said, "but I turned up in the South Pacific." Wounded three times, Cappy earned a battlefield commission and, after the war, served as an aide to General William F. Marquat.

As head of the joint U.S./Japan Goodwill Baseball Tour, Harada succeeded in getting the three major newspapers, *Asahi*, *Yomiuri* and the *Mainichi*, to cosponsor the Seals' tour. He was also responsible for securing permission from General MacArthur to raise the Japanese flag and play the national anthem for the first time in the postwar period during the tour's opening ceremonies. When the Japanese flag and the American flag were raised simultaneously, one of the officers present suggested to General MacArthur that Lieutenant Harada be court-martialed for having the Japanese flag raised alongside with the American flag. MacArthur responded that Harada had already asked him and that he had agreed that it should be done.

As an aide to General Marquat, Harada was responsible for rehabilitating many Japanese industries and companies, including trading, banking and insurance businesses. In the spring of 1950, he convinced Japanese baseball magnates to organize two leagues and conduct their own world series. At the same time, he organized a goodwill tour to Japan by Lefty O'Doul and Joe DiMaggio to conduct the first postwar baseball clinics for the professional baseball clubs in Japan. O'Doul and DiMaggio went together to Japan two times during the 1950s to coach Japanese players.

Lefty took another postwar team of big leaguers to Japan in 1951, the year of Joe DiMaggio's retirement, to play sixteen games against individual teams from the Japanese Central and Pacific Leagues. The team—O'Doul's All-Stars—included Joe DiMaggio, Joe's brother Dom, Billy Martin and a young left-handed pitcher named Mel Parnell, who had won eighteen games that year for the Boston Red Sox. Parnell was quoted as saying, "Watching Lefty operate was the highlight of the trip. On our arrival in Tokyo, you would have thought he was the emperor. Along our play route, a deafening chant was heard, 'Banzai O'Doul.'" O'Doul was most gracious in handling the crowd, and they showed their appreciation for what he had done for Japanese baseball.

Cappy Harada and Joe DiMaggio take the field at Korakuen Stadium in Tokyo, 1950. Always supportive of Japanese baseball, DiMaggio enjoyed his visits to Japan and was treated like royalty by the Japanese people. *Courtesy Cappy Harada.*

Once again, Japanese youngsters were enthralled. In a Catholic mission in Tokyo, the kids were preparing for confirmation. They were told that they had the privilege of adding a new name to the one they had received at baptism. Little Toshi couldn't think of a saint's name he wanted to adopt.

147

Joe DiMaggio has an opportunity to visit with American-born Japanese player Kenshi Zenimura (far left) and two of his Hiroshima Carp teammates. *Kenichi Zenimura collection.*

Japanese American baseball legend Kenichi Zenimura (center) meets up with Japanese Baseball Hall of Fame manager Shigeru Mizuhara and Cappy Harada in Fresno, California, during a 1953 tour of the mainland by the Yomiuri Giants. *Courtesy Masao Iriyama.*

"Why don't you choose Francis?" suggested the nun who was his teacher, for St. Francis de Sales. "Ahh," Toshi said. A few days later, the bishop was about to administer the sacrament. "And what is your confirmation name?" he asked. Toshi's face lit up. "San Francisco Seals," he said proudly.

In the spring of 1953, O'Doul, with the aid of Cappy Harada, organized the first spring-training camp in the United States for Japanese baseball clubs. The Yomiuri Giants trained in Santa Maria, California, and played exhibition games against the New York Giants, Chicago White Sox, St. Louis Browns and many Pacific Coast League teams. Before returning home, they won six out of eighteen games against major- and minor-league competition. O'Doul's impact was so far-reaching that he even helped influence the Japanese uniforms—in 1951, the Yomiuri Giants' uniform was almost identical to that worn by O'Doul when he played for the New York Giants in 1933 and 1934.

A historic first that took place during the Yomiuri Giants' spring-training camp in the United States was the appearance of Emmett Ashford, who became the first black umpire to work a professional game. Ashford, who went on to become a major-league umpire, got his professional start by working a game between the New York Giants and the Yomiuri Giants in Santa Maria. Cappy Harada was very proud to hire Emmett and give him an opportunity to pioneer this field.

In the fall of 1953, Harada organized the first New York Giants goodwill baseball tour of Japan and the Orient. After the tour, Horace Stoneham, the Giants' owner, appointed Harada as a scout and team representative for Japan and Asia. Harada had proven to be a very effective go-between because of his baseball expertise and savvy. In the spring of 1954, Harada led the Yomiuri Giants on a goodwill tour of Mexico, Panama, Colombia, the Dominican Republic, Cuba and the United States. That fall, he led the Giants on a goodwill tour of Australia and the Philippines despite anti-Japanese feelings. He succeeded in creating goodwill between the people of Japan and those of Australia and the Philippines through the medium of baseball.

Also that year, Joe DiMaggio and Marilyn Monroe were married, with Lefty O'Doul serving as Joe's best man. Because of the press and media attention, they asked their friend Cappy Harada to sponsor them to come to Japan for the newly wedded couple's honeymoon. Harada arranged for the three to come to Japan. This time O'Doul and DiMaggio would have the spotlight stolen away from them. Marilyn Monroe was a huge hit in Asia. She accompanied the former ballplayers wherever they went as they conducted batting clinics with the Japanese professional teams. Any doubt

Left: Marilyn Monroe and Joe DiMaggio arrive for their honeymoon in Japan in 1954 along with Lefty O'Doul and Cappy Harada. During the visit, Joe gave batting clinics to the Japanese professional teams, and Marilyn visited the troops stationed in Korea. *Courtesy Cappy Harada.*

Below: Joe DiMaggio stood out as a celebrity even when he was out of the limelight, as during this side trip with Marilyn Monroe to the remote Japanese countryside. *Courtesy Cappy Harada.*

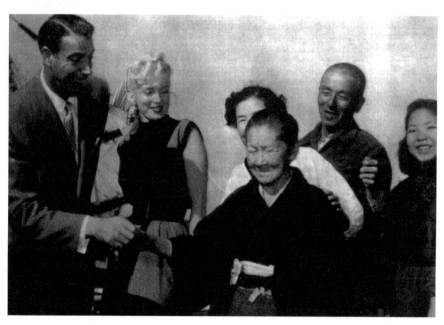

about which of the trio had the greatest news value was laid to rest one afternoon in the countryside. Joe and Marilyn had sneaked away from the prying eyes of the press and taken a three-hour train ride from Tokyo to a place where Joe intended to teach his bride some golf. Following one of their rounds of golf, the honeymooners decided to explore the countryside. A farmer recognized Marilyn Monroe first and then DiMaggio. He quickly spread the word around the farms that "Marilyn Monroe and her ball-playing husband were visiting the neighborhood!"

During this same trip, Monroe's agent took her on a side trip to entertain American troops in Korea. When the glamorous movie star returned from her trip to the U.S. army base, she told her husband, "Joe, you never heard such cheering." DiMaggio replied simply, "Yes, I have."

Also in the eventful year of 1953, the New York Giants and the Ed Lopat All-Stars toured Japan and competed with the pro teams. Baseball commissioner Ford Frick accompanied the teams. Upon his return to New York, Frick proclaimed that "the visits of the Giants and the Lopat team have resulted in more and better friendships between our nation and Japan.

Only the third Nisei to be inducted into Japan's Baseball Hall of Fame, Wally Yonamine, pictured here with the Yomiuri Giants, played for eleven years and coached and managed for an additional twenty-six years. *Courtesy Wally Yonamine.*

Superstars of the Postwar Period

Baseball was helping to heal the wounds of war in the United States as well. As racial restrictions and tensions finally relaxed in America, some of the top Nisei players took advantage of the changing times to play Division I college baseball as well as professional baseball in both the United States and Japan. Here are the stories of some of these Japanese American postwar stars.

The Zenimuras and Ben Mitsuyoshi

The 1953 season brought three Nisei to Japan from Fresno, California. Brothers Howard (Kenso) and Harvey (Kenshi) Zenimura played for the Hiroshima Carp, along with pitcher Ben Mitsuyoshi. Both Howard and Harvey had starred at Fresno State before signing with the professional Carp. Even as fourteen- and fifteen-year-olds, they had competed with men. Their father, Kenichi Zenimura, had devised a system that had no age requirements. If you were an "A" caliber player, you were at a semipro level, while "B" was high school level and "C" was junior high level. With this type of system, the only thing that mattered was playing ability, not age. Ben Mitsuyoshi was fresh from helping win a championship for his army team in Germany. As soon as he returned to the States, Kenichi Zenimura referred him to the Carp.

The Zenimuras and Mitsuyoshi left the small agricultural city of Fresno for Hiroshima, Japan. When they arrived at the Hiroshima train station, a huge crowd pressed forward to get a look at the American stars—100,000 fans lined the motorcade route to their hotel. "It was shocking to see so many people as we walked through the sea of bodies to get to the car," said Howard Zenimura. Harvey added, "I really wanted to do good for the team knowing that the city was sponsoring the ballclub and wasn't owned by a huge corporation."

During his 1954 tour of Japan, Joe DiMaggio took a liking to Harvey Zenimura because of his American roots and background. Harvey went on to become a two-time Central League all-star. In a series between the New York Giants and the Hiroshima Carp, Harvey batted over .400 and was presented with a batting trophy—a sewing machine. Past winners of the batting title had received a live pig and a live salmon.

Fibber Hirayama

When the atomic bomb burst over Hiroshima on August 6, 1945, Satoshi "Fibber" Hirayama was playing baseball in the Arizona sunshine at the Poston Relocation Center #2. Fibber said about his days in the camp, "There really wasn't much else to do but play baseball. The nearest town was twenty miles away, and we weren't allowed to go outside the barbed wire." Fibber was fifteen at the time. Three years earlier, he had been evicted from Exeter, California. One moment he was peddling his bicycle over the highways of Tulare County, and the next moment he was being picked up as a potential enemy alien. Their home and possessions sold, Fibber and his family took up residence in a barrack at Poston #2. A few days after the dropping of the bomb (residents of Hiroshima call it "the catastrophe"), the Hirayamas were permitted to return home. Before the war, Fibber had been the only Asian at Exeter High and had won admiration for his athletic skills. After honing his skills inside the Poston camp, he was ready to achieve not only acceptance but also distinction after the war. He was accepted at Fresno State College with a scholarship for tuition and a stipend of fifty dollars per month. He played football in the autumn and baseball in the spring. At only 150 pounds, pound for pound, he was the best halfback on the West Coast. He both ran and threw passes, and he was extremely quick and elusive. On defense, he was notably adept at intercepting passes. Talking about being hit by players who outweighed him by fifty to sixty pounds, Fibber said, "Nobody ever hit me real solid. I didn't mind hitting real hard, and come to think of it, I really didn't mind getting hit."

Fibber played for the Fresno State baseball teams from 1950 through 1952, twice being the captain. Fresno State's program was one of the strongest in the nation. In 1951, Fresno played against such major universities as the University of California, USC, Stanford, UCLA and Oregon. Its record was 31-9. In one season, Fibber stole seventy-six bases, and he stole five bases in the same game on three separate occasions. Those records stood for almost forty years until future major leaguer Tommy Goodwin broke the latter record.

In 1952, Fibber was signed by the Stockton Ports of the Pacific Coast League and played one year as a professional. He was looking forward to his future when Uncle Sam drafted him into the army. Fibber ended up serving two years at Ford Ord, California, and took this time to play army baseball. "We had good competition on the base, and a few guys went to the major leagues," said Fibber. After he served his military commitment, Fibber's former coach, Kenichi Zenimura, contacted him about joining the Hiroshima Carp and being reunited with the Zenimura brothers. In 1955, Fibber journeyed to Japan and became a member of the Carp.

An essayist writing for a Hiroshima magazine called *CARP* observed that Fibber had the "strongest shoulders of any Carp, and it is a tangible fact that he is the only Carp who can throw to home plate from the farthest reaches of the ball place." Fibber's arm was indeed legendary. During a 1951 tour

American-born Nisei Fibber Hirayama visits with Hall of Fame manager Casey Stengel during the New York Yankees' 1955 tour of Japan. Fibber managed a base hit off Yankee ace Whitey Ford. *Courtesy Fibber Hirayama.*

in Honolulu with the Fresno State team, he retired a runner at home with a heroic throw from 360 feet out. Writer Wallace Hirai maintained that "other than Joe DiMaggio, no player has come through with such a perfect strike from the outfield in the 25-year history of Honolulu Stadium."

From the first time he laced up his cleats with the Hiroshima Carp, according to veteran second baseman Jiro Kanayama, Fibber took charge. Kanayama recalls his astonishment when he returned to the dugout between innings one day and discovered that Fibber, who had run in from center field, was already sitting on the bench. Kanayama also began to quickly run off the field after innings. Fibber had a contagious passion, and he uplifted the entire Carp team. Many wanted to emulate him because of his fence-crashing pursuit of fly balls, his strong arm and his hard-nosed way of playing baseball.

Fibber's career in Japan included memorable encounters with touring major-league teams from the United States. "I'll never forget when the '55 Yankees came to Japan," he said. "My greatest thrill of playing the Yankees was getting a base hit off of Whitey Ford." In 1958, the St. Louis Cardinals toured the country with Hall of Famer Stan Musial. "We played them pretty tough," Hirayama remembered, "but they usually won by one run or so." Today, Hirayama splits his time between Fresno, Hiroshima and the Dominican Republic. He is a coach and scout in the Dominican Republic at the Hiroshima Carp Baseball Academy. He coaches and studies Dominican athletes, looking for the next player to advance to the professional level in Japan. "So many of these players here have the softest hands and strongest arms you will see," Fibber says. "That's why so many become middle infielders in the majors."

One prospect Fibber is very proud of became a major-league all-star: "Alfonso Soriano had the softest hands I had ever seen for an infielder." On Fibber's recommendation, the Carp signed Soriano to the major-league club in Hiroshima, and after two years he signed up with the New York Yankees and then the Chicago Cubs. Now he's back with the Yankees.

Jiro Nakamura and Hank Matsubu

It was another hot, windless day in the valley town of Bakersfield, California, in the summer of 1949. The baseball fans were chatting and fanning themselves, anticipating the start of the game. "Ladies and gentleman," the public address announcer intoned, "for the Modesto Reds, pitching today, Jiro Nakamura. Hank Matsubu catching." These words marked the appearance of the first all-Nisei battery in U.S. professional baseball history. Jiro Nakamura and Hank Matsubu had both been signed to professional contracts with the Modesto Reds, a Pittsburgh Pirates farm team. Babe Herman, the former Dodger star, was a Pirate scout when he saw Matsubu in action with the College of Idaho. Herman, who had signed such stellar performers as slugging Hall of Famer Ralph Kiner, wired his bosses about the Japanese American. The

In 1949, catcher Hank Matsubu was one of the first Nisei after the war to play professional baseball as a minor leaguer with the Modesto (California) Reds. Matsubu was offered an opportunity to play for the Yomiuri Giants, but he chose to retire instead. *Courtesy Hank Matsubu.*

championship College of Idaho team wound up that year's campaign with a record of 21-6. Matsubu hit .300 for the season.

Hank Matsubu was one of the many graduates of the internment school of baseball. A native of Corbett, Oregon, Hank was attending high school when the war broke out. He was relocated to the Minidoka, Idaho detention center. He played on the camp team as the catcher but also played virtually every other position at one time or another as well. He even pitched two one-hitters and won a no-hit game. At the age of seventeen, Hank was asked to coach the camp's high school team, which played exhibition games against outside teams from Twin Falls, Jerome, Rupert and Burley.

After being released from camp, the Matsubu family resettled in Payette, Idaho. The family worked the farm belt in the area, and Hank played with the town team. The team's baseball diamond sat on a rectangular football field. The left-field fence was more than 400 feet from home plate. However, it was only 280 feet down the right-field line and 305 to dead center. "I really started to salivate looking at the short center and right-field fences," said Hank.

Hank took advantage of the fences by going the opposite way with his hitting, and it proved to be a successful tactic. He concentrated on waiting on the ball as long as he could and, with his fast bat, would hit the inside part of the ball and drive it to center or right, many times over the fence. "We had a batboy on the team who was a pretty big kid," he remembered. "One of the players said that he hit a home run over the left-field fence. I couldn't believe the story because it looked like it was five hundred feet away. Later I found out the kid had been Hall of Famer Harmon Killebrew, and now I believe the story." Nineteen months in the special service division of the army followed, during which the twenty-one-year-old Hank caught on with the Fort Lewis Warriors. His catching and hitting paced the Warriors to the Sixth Army Championship. In three championship games, he hit .583 and batted in ten runs, earning Sixth Army Championship all-star honors. A month later, Matsubu signed his pro contract with the Modesto Reds. "I was at San Jose for my first at-bat," he related, "and I drove the ball to right centerfield for a base hit. What a great feeling that was. I thought I was on my way to hitting .500 in the pros."

After turning pro, Hank Matsubu gave voice to the aspirations shared by many postwar Nisei stars. "I have always had hopes of playing professional baseball," he said. "There has never been a Japanese American in the big leagues. It is my ambition to make that grade. Like heavyweight champion Joe Lewis and Sugar Ray Robinson, I just hope I can help my race to gain equal footing in sports as they have for theirs. I'm so proud I was able to help all our families on the battlefield as well as on the playing field."

Hank had become such a pronounced opposite-field hitter that Reds opponents sometimes employed the "Ted Williams shift" even though he was a right-handed batter. "The third baseman would be at shortstop, shortstop behind second base and the left fielder in center," he remembered. Hank would simply deposit the ball in the gap somewhere in right center anyway. Later, pitchers started hitting the inside corner of the plate, and Hank couldn't take the ball to the opposite field as much.

In 1949, under the recommendations of scouting agent Cappy Harada, Matsubu was offered a Japanese professional-league contract by Lefty O'Doul and the Yomiuri Giants. The Giants were interested in grooming an American catcher, and Hank fit the bill. Hank thought about the offer and weighed his options. Instead of going to Japan, he opted to settle down and marry his longtime sweetheart, Edna Hirabayashi. So ended Hank's aspirations of becoming possibly the first major-league baseball player of the Nisei generation.

A few weeks after signing Hank, the Modesto Reds signed up a second Nisei, Jiro Nakamura. Nakamura was nineteen years old and had been an outstanding pitcher for two years at San Mateo Junior College. In one season, he pitched and batted his team into the Northern California Junior College Championship. They lost the playoff, however, in a 2–0 pitchers' duel with Jim Sakamoto of Sacramento. Nakamura lost only one game during the season leading up to that final. His college success led to his historic role as half of the first all-Nisei battery.

POSTWAR BASEBALL AND RECONCILIATION

Nisei baseball pioneers in the postwar period were interlinked with the proud history and legacy of the United States, Japan, the Dominican Republic and many other countries across the globe. Individuals such as Lieutenant Cappy Harada, Wally Yonamine, Fibber Hirayama, the Zenimura brothers, Ben Mitsuyoshi, Hank Matsubu and Jiro Nakamura represent the scores of Nisei and American players who trail-blazed the path of reconstruction and reconciliation both in the United States and in Japan.

During the difficult resettlement period for Japanese Americans, baseball provided a way for former internees to reconnect with their communities and regions. As social conditions changed, diverse and integrated ethnic leagues started to emerge. Players like Eddie Takei, Bill Nishita, George Hinaga, Jim Sakamoto and many others began to make the minor-league ranks and hastened the day when Americans of all backgrounds could aspire to play professional ball.

In Japan, the aggressive American style of play that pioneering Nisei players displayed helped to change and elevate professional baseball. These players also helped to build a bridge across the Pacific that has since been crossed by professionals of both countries. The recent wave of world-class professional pitchers from Japan can be thankful that these pros of the postwar period prepared the way for them.

In the effort to rebuild relations between the United States and Japan, diplomats and politicians were overshadowed by such baseball missionaries as Lefty O'Doul, the San Francisco Seals and the major-league teams and stars who brought postwar goodwill tours to help heal the wounds of war. Another such emissary was Rod Dedeaux, former head coach of the University of Southern California baseball team. In 1955, Dedeaux made numerous tours with college athletes to compete with Japanese colleges on goodwill tours. In May 1996, the government of Japan presented Dedeaux with the Cordon Fourth Order of the Rising Sun in recognition of his efforts. Waseda University made Rod an honorary alumnus.

Baseball continues to provide a medium of communication as well as friendly competition between nations. In 1984, with the support of Peter O'Malley, then owner of the Los Angeles Dodgers, the Japanese Olympic baseball team competed at Dodger Stadium in a demonstration tournament. In the finals, Japan defeated the United States, thus proving that other countries could be competitive in Olympic baseball. O'Malley has been a strong proponent of international baseball and has even established a Dodger Academy in the Dominican Republic as well as scouting combines in Japan.

The O'Malley family has had a unique and positive relationship with the Nikkei community. Ike Ikuhara, a famous prewar Waseda University all-star baseball player in Japan, journeyed to America with the dream of working in professional baseball. He landed his first and only job as an assistant for Dodger Walter O'Malley. Ike's son-in-law Acey Kohrogi would later work with Peter O'Malley in the same capacity and operated as their scout in Asia. Also part of the Dodger organization was Nisei Nobi Kawano, who served as the Dodger's clubhouse manager for thirty-one years. Additionally, Nobi's brother, Yosh, worked with the Chicago Cubs for sixty years, and the Cubs recently named their clubhouse after him.

These new missionaries of baseball have followed in the footsteps of such earlier emissaries as Horace Wilson and Tillie Shafer. They have shown once again that a bat and a ball can do more than rifles and bullets to forge relations between countries that share an interest in sports.

Chapter 8

SANSEI, YONSEI, SHIN ISSEI AND JAPANESE NATIONALS STEP UP TO THE PLATE

When they announced my name, I heard this loud scream. I had what Hawaiians call "chicken skin" running out to the mound. It was incredible seeing fifty thousand fans out there cheering you on.
—Onan Masaoka

In the 1950s musical *Damn Yankees*, ballplayers worn down by years of defeat sing an anthem of hope, "You Gotta Have Heart." Perhaps no group in America was in a better position to appreciate the message of the song than Japanese Americans. The first generation of Japanese Americans, the Issei, had come to the United States with high ambitions to tackle a fresh beginning in a land filled with opportunity. The bitter reality was that when they came to the mainland, they faced hard labor, restrictive laws and widespread xenophobia. Still, they persisted, slowly building up their fortunes, only to see their empires crash in the debilitating Depression of the 1930s. Then, just as they were getting on their feet again, Japanese assets in the United States were frozen by presidential order in 1941. Five months later, war was declared on Japan, and once again the Issei and their families lost everything as they were herded into relocation centers and, ultimately, detention camps.

For the Nisei, the resettlement period after one war in some ways paralleled in America. The average age of the Nisei during the war was twenty-four. After the war, the majority of Nisei became heads of households. Like their parents before them, they were starting over from scratch. Most Japanese American

Japanese national pitching sensation Hideo Nomo opened the door for many Japanese pitchers playing in the major leagues today. Nomo was National League Rookie of the Year with the Los Angeles Dodgers in 1995 and pitched a no-hitter against the Colorado Rockies at Coors Field on September 17, 1997. *Courtesy Los Angeles Dodgers.*

families never recovered the homes or businesses they had lost during the internment because the deeds had passed to new owners. Their property had been sold for ten cents on the dollar. A few lucky families had trusted neighbors who oversaw their belongings and property, but for most Japanese Americans, resettlement was another crusade for survival. Physically, mentally and spiritually, the Issei could not shoulder another rebuilding process. Their children would have to bear the burden of starting over.

The Nisei were the bridge from the prewar years to the very different society of postwar America. Their children and their grandchildren (the Sansei and Yonsei generations) would come of age in a changed country, one that was becoming increasingly the land of opportunity the Issei had dreamed of, both on and off the ball field. By the 1990s, these Americans of Japanese descent would be joined in the major leagues by a new postwar wave of arrivals from the ancestral country of Japan—the Shin Issei.

THE LAST HURRAH OF THE NISEI

After the war, the thousands of Japanese Americans who were displaced because of internment took up the challenge of making a reentry into American society. Many families moved into Euro-American neighborhoods across the country to start over in a new, more diverse America. They soon became known for their hard work and exemplary behavior. In April 1955, an article by Demaree Bess entitled "California's Amazing Japanese" appeared in the *Saturday Evening Post*. The article noted, "The Japanese residents of California have lifted themselves higher in a few postwar years than they did in the preceding half century, and the agitation against them has almost silenced. They are the model minority."

As the Nisei returned to society, they reestablished baseball teams and leagues, and for a time, Japanese American baseball was once again a thriving pastime. Nisei legends now began to manage and coach their children, the Sanseis. Teams mushroomed all throughout California. The all-powerful prewar JAU (Japanese Athletic Union), which had been founded in the 1930s, spawned the Little Tokyo Giants from Los Angeles, the LA Tigers, the Nichiren Orions and Gardena FOR (Friends of Richard). Up north, the Stockton Asahi, the San Francisco Traders and the Sacramento All-Stars were some of the powerhouse teams of the postwar era.

In 1953, the Sacramento Valley Nisei All-Stars won the first Nisei championship after the war by defeating Lodi. The Placer Japanese American Citizens League (JACL) claimed the crown the following year, stopping the Nisei Trading club (a Los Angeles company-sponsored team) in the finals. In 1955, the Placer JACL repeated as champions, this time defeating the San Jose Zebras. Nisei Trading rose to the top in 1956 as San Jose once again lost in the finals. Northern California reclaimed the honors in 1957 when the San Francisco Hawks downed the Little Tokyo Giants of Los Angeles for the championship. Carlton Hanta was named MVP of the championship tournament that season. The following year, he signed with the Nankai Hawks and went on to play pro ball in Japan for five years. In 1958, Nisei Trading edged the Little Tokyo Giants 6–5. The following year, Mayhew, California, defeated San Francisco in the seventh annual tournament. In 1960, the Little Tokyo Giants avenged their 1958 defeat by downing Nisei Trading in a tournament held in Glendale.

During this period, as related in the last chapter, a number of Nisei players were making inroads in professional baseball, including Wally Yonamine with the Salt Lake City Bees, Fibber Hirayama with the Stockton Ports and Jiro Nakamura and Hank Matsubu with the Modesto Reds. San Jose's George Hinaga played for a team in Vancouver, and Bill Nishita played for

Frank (left) and Henry Ota with their father, Harry. Both brothers captained their team at Dartmouth in 1965. Henry was captain of the varsity team, and Frank captained the freshman squad. *Courtesy Henry Ota.*

Montreal. Ed Takei played in Oakland and Oregon before going on to a pro career in Japan. Other Nisei pros in Japan included Yonamine, Hirayama, the Zenimura brothers and Carlton Hanta. These Nisei pioneers paved the way for future generations of Japanese Americans to join the mainstream. The Nisei's last hurrah marked the transition to a time of increasing integration, assimilation and opportunity for Japanese Americans.

THE POSTWAR GENERATION

The Nisei now had children, who would be called the Sansei, or third generation of Japanese Americans. Most Sansei were born between the years 1945 and 1965, the baby boom period. Although nearly all Sansei shared a common experience in culture, the Sansei generation would be characterized by its extreme diversity. Nisei parents stressed the importance of education and professional aspirations to the Sansei generation, and most of their children accepted these professional goals. However, while some Sansei retained a strong Japanese American or Asian American identity, others felt little identification with other Japanese Americans. As compared with Nisei, fewer Sansei lived in Japanese American communities, and fewer still lived in rural areas. Many did not have Japanese American friends in school, and because of their interaction with Americans of other backgrounds, they did not connect with their culture. Many married outside their race, and their children would be called "Hapa" (half Japanese). By the 1960s, a cultural revolution was beginning in which ethnic groups of all colors were both seeking their identities and attempting to claim their place in the mainstream culture. Although some Sansei were active in the political movements of the 1960s, including the so-called Asian American Movement, others were apolitical. Members of the Sansei generation were out to get a foothold in American society and focused on professional careers to better themselves and their lifestyle. Like most of their Nisei parents, they turned the page on the negative past and looked forward to a new chapter of acclimation and acculturation in postwar America.

This new approach extended to baseball. Many of the pioneers of Japanese American baseball have considered the 1920s and 1930s the golden years of Japanese American baseball, but they would encounter resistance and objections from members of the Sansei generation who played college and minor-league ball in the 1960s. Encouraged by their parents to commit themselves to college educations and to gain professional status in mainstream America, Sansei enrolled in Division I colleges throughout the country, and it was only natural that they took advantage of the opportunity to play baseball in this new environment. After all, the sport had been inbred into them through the experiences of their parents and grandparents. Whether baseball was played in exclusively Japanese American leagues or in integrated college and professional leagues, it was a positive aspect of life that spanned the generations.

Nisei legends now began to manage and coach their children, the Sansei. In many communities, Sansei teams and leagues sprouted up, beginning new rivalries similar to those of the prewar Nisei generation. In the Sansei leagues, there were Division I and college-level athletes who were sometimes sponsored by companies or individuals. Most, however, were content with the fellowship, the competitions and the networking opportunities and were not paid sponsorships for meals and expenses.

In 1961, the Fresno Sansei captured their first state championship. Eddie Miyamoto won the MVP award, while teammate Kat Shitanishi received the prize for the tournament's top hitter. The Fresno Sansei won again in 1962. In 1963, Gardena FOR (Friends of Richard) hosted the state tournament and was defeated by the Little Tokyo Giants in the finals. Most of the players on these teams, in addition to playing within their subcultural tournaments and leagues, played on integrated college-level teams. Their level of expertise, specialized knowledge and athletic ability rivaled those of the Nisei stars of the prewar years.

In 1965, brothers Henry and Frank Ota traveled to the East Coast to play for the Dartmouth College baseball program in the Ivy League. Henry and Frank had both played for Gardena High School and also with the Sansei leagues in Los Angeles. The young men's father, Harry Ota, was very proud that his two sons both became captains of Dartmouth baseball teams, Henry for the varsity squad and Frank for the freshman team. Even in the mid-1960s, however, prejudice presented challenges for Japanese Americans. Henry recalled, "I remember one time where we went to play Old Dominion in Hartford, Vermont. I was the first baseman, and in between innings I was throwing the balls to the infield, and I could hear these racial slurs directed at me. They would call me Charlie Chan or Chinaman, and here I was Japanese American. As I threw the ball to my second baseman, third baseman and shortstop, each time they would deliberately throw over my head and into the stands at spectators who were catcalling me at first base. The coach called us into the dugout and said, 'We will never come back here and play again, but you guys don't lower yourselves by trying to throw the baseballs at the fans," said Henry. While the fans' behavior was lamentable, Henry added that "it really made me feel good that my teammates were backing me up."

The Otas' success at Dartmouth reflected the growing participation of Sansei players in college competition. Ets Yoshiyama, a member of the famed Oliver's Club in Los Angeles, recalled Nisei college players who paved the way: "There were many college baseball stars who were Japanese American— June and Kay Miyagawa of Harvard, Billy Shundo from the University of Southern California, Joe Suski and Patrick Okura at UCLA, Jim Yamaguchi at Northwestern, Paul Yazaki from Notre Dame, Kiyo Nogami and Sam Rokutani at Cal Berkeley, Bill Kajikawa at Arizona State, Pat Nagano at Stanford, Jake Kakuuchi, Brooks Iwakiri, Zuke Tanaka, George Goto…they took care of business academically and on the baseball diamond."

MAKING "THE SHOW"

The odds against any player's making it to the major leagues are overwhelming. The way to the majors is an unbelievable funnel that begins with thousands upon thousands of kids all over the country who dream of going to "The Show" someday and ends with only the most select few. For Japanese Americans, as well as for players from Japan, the dream was out of reach for many years—even if they had the necessary talent and drive. Nisei pioneers blazed the trail, Sansei players extended it and now Yonsei (fourth-generation) stars are beginning to arrive in baseball's promised land.

Baseball Executive Cappy Harada

One of the first Japanese Americans to break into the big leagues was Nisei Cappy Harada, the former aide to General Douglas MacArthur during the postwar occupation of Japan. Cappy's achievements in Japan were so striking that he was offered the position of baseball commissioner. Cappy, however, said that the post should be given to a native Japanese. The late Matsutaro Shoriki took the job and became known as the father of Japanese professional baseball.

Meanwhile, after helping to rebuild Japanese baseball as well as the "bridge across the Pacific," Cappy Harada became a scout and special assistant to Horace Stoneham, owner of the San Francisco Giants. It was Cappy who signed a pitcher from the Nankai Hawks named Masanori Murakami, the first player from Japan to play major-league baseball in the United States. Murakami didn't come over originally to play in the majors. The San Francisco team offered to bring him to the States in 1963 to learn the American way of baseball with the minor-league Fresno Giants. After watching his incredible progress, the big club called him up as a relief pitcher for San Francisco. Murakami posted a 4-1 record as a reliever. A prolific strikeout pitcher, he chalked up one hundred strikeouts in only 89 1/3 innings during his two-year stint with San Francisco, walking just twenty-three hitters. He proved to be one of the great success stories of the 1965 season, which was climaxed by a Murakami Day at Candlestick Park. Close to thirty thousand fans gave a big hand to the first Japanese player to make it to the U.S. big leagues. It would be thirty years before another player from Japan signed with a major-league team.

Signing Masanori Murakami was only one of the highlights of Cappy Harada's career in professional baseball. While he was working for the Giants, Cappy was offered the position of general manager of the minor-league Lodi Crushers. In his first year in this capacity, he received the Sporting News Class

A Executive of the Year Award. "Always do something for somebody and live by the golden rule—that's my approach," said Harada. The Crushers were part of the Chicago Cubs farm system. One of the players the Cubs assigned to Lodi was self-taught pitcher Lee Meyers, who announced before being moved from the Texas League to Lodi that he had secretly married Mamie Van Doren, the blonde bombshell of Hollywood movie and TV notoriety. When it was announced that Van Doren could be seen among the spectators at Lodi home games, thousands packed the park to get a glimpse of her.

Cappy's savvy as a promoter as well as a general manager helped boost attendance at the ballpark to record levels and brought the community of Lodi a proud landmark. Harada stayed as the general manager for one more year before returning to the Giants, where he continued to serve as special assignment executive under Horace Stoneham for twenty-three years.

Kat Shitanishi

About one hundred miles south of Lodi, a farm kid had advanced up the baseball ladder in youth leagues in the small community of Madera. At the end of his high school career, his skill as an infielder caught the attention of a local powerhouse baseball college, Fresno State. Katsu (Kat) Shitanishi quickly became an all-conference baseball player for the Fresno State Bulldogs as well as the team captain. The talented Sansei was then drafted by the Boston Red Sox and played in the minor leagues with future big-league stars Carlton Fisk, Graig Nettles and Amos Otis.

Every year, Kat escalated his baseball stock and advanced to a higher-level team. He spent his first year at Oneonta, New York; his second at Greenville, South Carolina; and his third at Winston-Salem, North Carolina. He was a good hitter, a sure-handed infielder and the leading base stealer for every team on which he played. One road trip in North Carolina was especially traumatic for the popular second baseman. "All the ballplayers were having a few drinks in this bar," Kat related, "and this drunk looked over at me and said, 'We killed your people in the war.' I must have said something back to him, and he came at me with a bottle. Before anything happened, my teammates grabbed him and we all left. I know most of the residents in this area had never laid eyes on a Japanese American before. I could almost feel people watching me. But I was a young, confident ballplayer who was performance-driven." Kat did perform on the field, and he developed quite

Kat Shitanishi (pictured here, second from left, with several of his Oneonta Red Sox teammates) played minor-league baseball for five seasons and for five different organizations. He had the opportunity to play with future major leaguers like Hall of Famer Carlton Fisk, Craig Nettles and Amos Otis (far right). *Courtesy Kat Shitanishi.*

a following. "I noticed none of the blacks in the audience would ever sit directly behind the backstop; they would sit in the bleachers next to our dugout. I was one of their favorite players till we signed our first black player, Jimmy Walker, and their support shifted real quick," said Kat. Even in the 1960s, the chasm of prejudice still affected Sansei ballplayers.

The next stop for Kat was Pawtucket, Rhode Island. After a successful season there, he was sent up to the Pittsfield, Massachusetts team, one step away from his major-league dream. Kat recalled, "Our uniforms were the hand-me-downs from the big-league club. If I would have known he would be a Hall of Famer, I would have taken Ted Williams' number nine more often." During the middle of the season, Kat was taken out on a double play, injuring his knee. During his recovery period, he would play one game and rest two. At the end of the season, he had to make a career decision. "Once you get one step away from the major-league level, you pretty much know who you have to compete with to get the job," said Kat. "I knew it would take time for me to crack the lineup, and my injury was slowing my performance down. On those long road trips on the bus, I had time to reflect on what I'd do after baseball." Kat decided to retire that year and end his professional baseball aspirations. Although his journey stopped just short of the promised land, Kat was grateful for his experience: "I was an introvert before playing pro ball. Baseball allowed me to deal with people and gave me a winning attitude and opened me up toward life. I met some great people in baseball and have fond memories."

In the 1960s, Kat Shitanishi had the chance to break into the big leagues with the Red Sox before his injury put an end to his career. It wouldn't be until the late '60s that the first Japanese American would arrive in the major leagues.

Ryan Kurosaki

Many boys growing up in the village of Kaimuki, Hawaii, had dreams of one day becoming either a major-league baseball player or a fireman. Ryan Kurosaki fulfilled both dreams—after a successful baseball career, he retired into active service as a fireman in Benton, Arkansas.

When Ryan was growing up, his father, Katsuto, would coach his sons and take them to American Japanese Association games to watch his favorite team, the Islanders. "I was one of the knothole-gang kids that would just watch and dream of playing one day like the big kids," Ryan recalled. Ryan's brother Neal eventually played college ball with the University of Hawaii; Ryan would shoot for the stars and become the first Japanese American pitcher to play in the major leagues.

At Kalani High School, Ryan helped his team win the high school state championship in 1970. Ryan became the ace of the Kalani Falcons' pitching staff that year, going 6-0 with a 1.68 earned run average. "Kurosaki had a wicked breaking pitch," remembered former teammate Steve Kimura. Another teammate was Lenn Sakata, who would later play eleven seasons in the major leagues. "I have lots of memories, good memories, of pitching for that team," Ryan said. "When looking back, it was a great high school team." He added that playing for the Kalani coaches, Herb Okumura and Ralph Takeda, was a great learning experience. That championship season became a springboard to success at the collegiate level and beyond.

On a full scholarship at Nebraska from 1971 to 1973, Ryan became a big winner for the collegiate team. The Cornhuskers were nationally recognized

Relief pitcher Ryan Kurosaki was the first Sansei to reach the major leagues when he joined the St. Louis Cardinals and Hall of Famers Bob Gibson and Lou Brock. *Courtesy Ryan Kurosaki.*

as a powerhouse football school, not for their baseball program. Only two baseball scholarships were offered by the school, and Ryan received one of them. A major breakthrough in exposure came while playing semipro ball in Liberal, Kansas, during the summer of 1973. Kurosaki was spotted by a St. Louis scout when he pitched in a National Baseball Congress tournament. This tournament was a great showcase for college players, and scouts were everywhere. Kurosaki was named the MVP, racking up a 25-0 record. The following year, he returned to the tournament, but despite his domination over opposing teams, no offers came his way. "Guys were getting signed left and right, but no one wanted to talk to me," Kurosaki said. Finally, Byron Humphreys of the Cardinals signed Ryan for $6,000, and his professional stint began.

Ryan played in the California League for one year and then was brought up to the Arkansas Travelers squad, a minor-league team of the Cardinals. "At every level I played at, I was pretty successful," Kurosaki said. He began the 1975 season as a relief pitcher for the Travelers and quickly became the top stopper in the league, compiling a 4-0 record with four saves and no earned runs allowed in twenty-one innings. His dream of pitching in the majors became a reality when he was called up to the Cardinals in May. On May 20, 1975, he made his big-league debut when he was summoned from the Cardinals' bullpen to stop a San Diego threat. He pitched one and two-thirds innings of shutout relief, striking out one batter and walking three. "I was just blessed to become the first player of my ancestry to reach the big leagues," he said. Kurosaki answered the bullpen call seven times and pitched thirteen innings for the Cardinals that season. He had no decisions and no saves. That turned out to be his entire major-league career. Although it was brief, Kurosaki came away with vivid memories and strong feelings. "I was in awe when I reported," he recalled. "I walked into the locker room, and here are my teammates, Lou Brock and Bob Gibson," both of whom are now in the Hall of Fame. "Ron Fairly, a veteran player at first base, was my roommate on the road, and I learned a lot from him also." The lack of everyday work as a starter might have contributed to a slight injury that led to rehabilitation in AA ball and in the Mexican winter leagues. Like many players faced with rehabilitation and recovery, Ryan had to decide whether he could maintain a world-class level of baseball. Having made it to a level that most kids can only dream about, Ryan weighed his options and ended his career with the Hermosillo Seals in Mexico.

"Today, the players are bigger, stronger and faster, but they have some problems. They don't have the same reverence for the game that we had," Ryan says. Of his life as a Denton, Arkansas fireman, he observes, "Putting out fires in the real world is a lot riskier than [being] out on the major-league diamonds for the St. Louis Cardinals."

Lenn Sakata

Ryan Kurosaki's high school teammate Lenn Sakata was a multitalented utility player at every position except pitcher who could also hit for power. Like Ryan, he followed a course that took him to the major leagues. Lenn took a little longer to get there, but he stayed much longer once he arrived.

Lenn grew up in Honolulu. Melvin and Marge Sakata were very proud of their only child, who lived for baseball. "I was only four or five, and my dad would take me to watch these baseball games. I was mesmerized, and I knew then that's what I wanted to be—a baseball player," recalled Sakata. He later became the batboy for the famed Asahi. His uncle Jack Ladra played for the Asahi and would eventually play seven years for the major-league Toei Flyers in Tokyo.

Having settled on his dream, Lenn played through the ranks of the youth leagues. The turning point in his career came in high school when his dad pulled him aside and said, "You'd better start lifting weights if you are going to compete at higher levels." The elder Sakata's wisdom proved to be a success, as Lenn got bigger and stronger. He helped his high school team win two state championships and numerous contests against American Legion teams.

Veteran major leaguer Sansei Lenn Sakata played eleven seasons with the Milwaukee Brewers, Baltimore Orioles, Oakland A's and New York Yankees. He was a member of the Orioles World Series team in 1983, has coached in Japan and manages the Class A San Jose Giants. *Courtesy* Baltimore Sun.

When college baseball offers did not materialize, Lenn chose to enroll at the Treasure Valley Community College in Oregon. After two prosperous seasons, he attended Gonzaga University in Spokane, Washington, on a baseball scholarship. One game at Gonzaga caught the attention of Dick Wilson, a scout for the Giants. Lenn had a triple and a home run in that game. Afterward, the scout talked to Lenn about a future pro career. A short while later, the San Diego Padres drafted Lenn in the fifth round, but they offered him no money to sign. Lenn played another year at Gonzaga and then was drafted in the first round by the Milwaukee Brewers. In 1976, he reported to the Spokane Indians of the Pacific Coast League. One huge highlight for Lenn was returning to the islands to play against the Islanders at Aloha Stadium in front of friends and family. "It was a great experience. I was nervous at first but settled down and even hit a home run in one of the games," he recalled. Lenn characterized many of the hardships a ballplayer goes through as dues paying. "You have to cope with and adjust to all the injuries and mental preparations for each game and get an opportunity to play." He added, "To become successful in baseball, one has to be at the right place at the right time." He became the number-three batter in the lineup, and at the end of the season, he was selected as the second baseman on the PCL all-star team.

In 1977, Lenn's father, Melvin, passed away. "Some of my dad's co-workers told me how proud he was of my pro career. My dad would never verbally tell me these things, but I knew he was because he loved baseball. It was a serious awakening and realization for me not to have my dad around. He never got to see me play major-league baseball, but I know he was with me in spirit."

One of Lenn's coaches in AAA was the "Man Mountain," former major-league star Frank Howard, who had played in Japan for the Taiheiyo Club Lions in 1974. Lenn recalled taking infield with Howard coaching: "Frank was huge and would hit the ball as hard as he could during infield. I would gobble them up not making any errors, and I think he liked that."

In July 1977, Lenn's years of preparation paid off when he was notified to report to the Milwaukee Brewers. He played in fifty-three games that first year but saw little action with the Brewers the next two seasons. By 1980, he was playing for the Baltimore Orioles. A bit of poetic justice happened that season when the Orioles played Milwaukee. Lenn came in to pinch-hit and ripped a double to win the game for Baltimore. "I really thrived being put into those situations where you have to come through for the team," Lenn said. "What a feeling it is when you see the crowd giving you a standing ovation!"

In 1983, Lenn played a key role in one of the most exciting comebacks in Orioles history. On August 24, the Toronto Blue Jays led the Orioles 4–3 in the top of the tenth. Baltimore reliever Tippy Martinez had not picked off a runner in three years. That was about to change with career infielder Lenn Sakata behind the plate. With pinch hitters and runners depleting the bench, two of the Orioles outfielders were playing at second and third, while Lenn was pressed into duty as a catcher for the first and only time in his major-league career. A single by Barry Bonnell of the Blue Jays brought Martinez into the game with no one out. With an emergency catcher in the game for the Orioles, things did not look good. "My thoughts were focused on how to get out of the situation without going to home," Martinez would say afterward. "With my being a breaking-ball pitcher, the chances of Lenn Sakata catching a ball was slim and none." Fortunately for the Orioles, Bonnell left first too soon and was tagged out in a rundown near second. One out. After walking pinch hitter Dave Collins, the ever-crafty Martinez worked his magic to quickly pick him off as well. Two outs. The next batter, Willie Upshaw, singled, but then he, too, was caught napping on the bases! Three outs on pickoffs squelched the Blue

Jays threat and put a dramatic end to Tippy's three-year streak of zero pickoffs. In the bottom half of the inning, Cal Ripken came up to bat for Baltimore and hit one out of the park to tie the game. The next batter grounded out, and the following batter struck out. With two outs and the game tied, Lenn Sakata walked up to the plate on legs that were fatigued from his catching stint. Blue Jays pitcher Cliff Johnson was ready to close out the inning. "I was thinking about getting a single to keep the rally going," Lenn recalled. "Johnson hung a slider up, and I was out in front of the ball. Whack! I pulled it for a line drive, and it hooked just inside the left field foul pole for a home run to end the game! It was a great victory that gave us momentum to go on to win our division." In fact, that year Lenn and his Orioles teammates went on to win the pennant and the World Series.

At the end of 1985, Lenn was traded to the Oakland A's. He played briefly for the A's in 1986 before being traded to the New York Yankees. With the Yankees in 1987, Lenn hit two home runs, one a game winner against the Chicago White Sox. Hampered by a lingering ankle injury, Lenn called it quits after the 1987 season, bringing to an end an eleven-year, 565-game career in the majors.

Major-league baseball is a small fraternity that prides itself on promoting from within. Players who have competed at this level are a distinct minority. Only 2 percent of all players drafted by professional teams ever make it to the major leagues. When coaching jobs open up, veterans with more than ten years of experience—a still more exclusive group—usually are the first to be considered.

The same year that Lenn Sakata retired as a player ended up being the year he started coaching. The Oakland A's brought him on board in 1987, and in 1988, he was assigned to a managerial position with the Southern Oregon team in Medford, Oregon. "It was like déjà vu coming back to the exact ball field that I played on as an American Legion player," said Sakata. He went on to coach and manage for three years with the California Angels organization at the AAA level in the summer, while the Hawaiian winter league would call on him to manage the Honolulu Sharks. From 1995 to 1998, Lenn worked in Japan managing the minor-league team of the Chiba Lotte Marines. Future New York Mets manager Bobby Valentine was up at the major-league level with the Marines. In 1999, Lenn returned to the mainland to manage the minor-league San Jose Giants.

Lenn Sakata was a veteran major leaguer who helped one of his teams get to the top of the mountain and win a World Series before going on to manage professionally in the United States and Japan. "I have been very fortunate to stay in the game this long and meet so many different people and broaden my perceptions of race relations," Sakata says. "I have traveled and played all over the world in countries like Nicaragua, the Dominican Republic, Mexico and Japan." Wherever Lenn goes in the future, he has earned his stripes as a major-league veteran and as a manager with experience on both sides of the Pacific. He never had a nickname during his playing days, but "Ambassador" Sakata has a nice ring to it.

Sansei players Ryan Kurosaki, Lenn Sakata, Mike Lum and Giants pitcher Atlee Hammaker pioneered the way for Japanese Americans at the major-league level. Sixteen years after Ryan Kurosaki's debut, the first member of the fourth generation (Yonsei) would step up and make it into "The Show."

Don Wakamatsu

Don Wakamatsu, the first Yonsei big leaguer, was born on February 22, 1963, in Hood River, Oregon. His great-grandparents were fruit growers from Fukuoka, Japan. His grandparents were also farmers, while his mother, Ruth, was a dental assistant and his father, James, was an ironworker superintendent. Don played all the youth sports, starting with Little League in Oakland, California. "I was the Baby Huey of my teams. I was bigger than everyone and usually slower, too," he remembered. Don also played for the Buddhist church teams as a youth and remembers going to his first big-league ballgame at the age of ten. "A neighbor of ours took us local kids to an Oakland A's game. This was when they were world champions. Walking into the stadium and seeing the field was an awesome sight. That's when you really start dreaming about being a major leaguer."

The Burkovich furniture store was a sponsor of the under-fifteen all-stars in the Oakland area. Ray Luce, the coach of the team, was always looking for young talent to showcase his team. Don remembers, "We would play almost one hundred games in the summertime, sometimes playing two double-headers in one day. Ray pretty much figured we were all-stars and let us just play. Sometimes I'd even catch him napping in the dugout. But it gave us great opportunities to get as many at-bats as possible." As he grew older and stronger, Don filled out his frame with muscle and gained speed. He became an all-star at Hayward High School, where coach Jim Bisenius was a major influence. "These were real important times in your life because of recruiters and scouts. Jim always put in a good word for me, and it made a difference,"

The first Yonsei player to reach the major leagues was Don Wakamatsu, who was an all-American and teammate of Barry Bonds at Arizona State University. With the Chicago White Sox, Wakamatsu was the personal catcher for knuckleballer Charlie Hough, and he was Class A minor-league Manager of the Year in 1998 in the Arizona Diamondbacks organization. He was named manager of the Seattle Mariners in 2008. *Courtesy Don Wakamatsu.*

said Don. After graduation, Don attended Arizona State University on a scholarship. Head coach Jim Brock and catching coach Gary Tuck went to work refining Don's skills. In his junior year, he was named to the All-Pac 10 team. "Not only did I have great coaches," Don recalled, "but I also played with some outstanding athletes. Barry Bonds was on our team, and Oddibe McDowell was a great player. We were stacked."

All the hard work finally paid off when Don received a telegram and a phone call informing him that he had been chosen in the tenth round of the major-league draft by the Chicago White Sox. Don started his journey to the majors in the Billings, Montana rookie league. He then went to Florida's class A league for two years before being promoted to the AA level in Chattanooga, Tennessee. His last stop before the majors was in AAA ball in Vancouver. After six years of minor-league baseball, Don made it to the White Sox in 1991. "When you decide you want to make baseball a professional career, success does not come easy. You have to have a tremendous work ethic, handle pressure, be very businesslike in your approach and have the natural ability," he said.

Don credits White Sox catching coach Jeff Torborg with being a major influence early in his career. One of his special moments with the Sox was being told by star catcher Carlton Fisk not to be anxious about getting his first major-league hit. Fisk had gone 0 for 25 before getting his first hit. He needn't have worried about the Sox rookie. Don's first at-bat was against the Anaheim Angels. Don jumped on a slider down and away and drove it to right field for his first big-league hit. "After getting the hit, Dave Winfield on the other team tapped me on the shin guard and said, 'I hope you get two thousand more.' He was a classy guy," said Don. Another milestone was watching runner Dave Henderson take off from first base and then setting up and firing a rope to second to throw him out. Throwing out base stealers when knuckleball artist Charlie Hough is fluttering pitches at you can be an adventure for many catchers. Unfortunately, the rigors of the game caught up with Don, and elbow surgery plus a foot injury slowed his progress dramatically. During Don's rehab in the minors, he ended up being a player-coach. Don enjoyed the duties of coaching, and word about his skills led to a new opportunity when the expansion Arizona Diamondbacks began seeking out candidates for new coaching positions. General manager Joe Garagiola Jr. and manager Buck Showalter met with Don and chose him as a minor-league manager in 1998. His first year in the Arizona organization brought him the Manager of the Year award for the California League. Don's parents once asked when he was going to take on a straight job. Don's response was, "I haven't had to work a day yet—why start now? I have played baseball my whole life. I'm good at this, and I have never had to change jobs." In 1999, Don began managing the AA El Paso Diablos, another Diamondbacks farm team. As the elder statesman for the young players coming up, Don shares his thoughts and experiences along with his love of the game. "You're on the bus for fifteen to sixteen hours, sometimes until three o'clock in the morning. Sometimes five players have to share one room. But you get to see the world, experience the crowd cheering you on and get paid for playing a game you have loved since you were a kid. I still love baseball and intend to for a long time."

In 2008, Don became the first Asian American to manage in the big leagues with the Seattle Mariners. Preparing for the upcoming season, he visited his grandparents in Hood River, Oregon. The house they lived in was built from wood at the Tule Lake, California concentration camp that they purchased on their departure. "To sit in their home that once was a barracks still gives me goose bumps knowing the hardship they went through to give me a better life and opportunity," said Don. Meanwhile, he and his wife, Laura, have three children who are Gosei (fifth generation). If another of Don's wishes comes true, one of his sons will one day take the field as the major leagues' first Gosei player.

FROM NOMO-MANIA TO ICHIRO TO MASAHIRO TANAKA: JAPANESE NATIONALS ARRIVE IN THE MAJORS

A new wave of Japanese began to arrive in 1995 with the celebrated arrival of pitcher Hideo Nomo. The young hurler from Osaka arrived at a time when relations between the United States and Japan were strained and reminiscent of the trade imbalance that preceded World War II. Hideo displayed his ambassadorship and his unique ability on the playing fields with the Los Angeles Dodgers, and "Nomo-mania" was launched. He captivated Japanese nationals as well as Japanese Americans around the country, and he changed the perceptions of Americans about Japanese players coming to the United States.

Nomo had an immediate impact in the major leagues, becoming the Rookie of the Year with the Dodger club. Two years later, on September 17, 1997, he accomplished a milestone for any major-league pitcher by throwing a no-hit game in the all-time hitter's paradise, Coors Field in Denver. Much like Jackie Robinson, Nomo crossed over an ethnic divide and had a huge impact on an audience that was initially unsure of his abilities and his intentions but was won over because of his playing skills and pioneering efforts. Tommy Lasorda said, "Nomo was to the Japanese people what Jackie Robinson was to the blacks. If Jackie Robinson failed as a player, that would have denied a lot of black players opportunities. If Nomo failed as a player, then Japanese baseball would have said, 'We're not there yet.'"

Nomo opened up the door for other Japanese ballplayers such as Shigetoshi Hasegawa, who caught on with the Anaheim Angels; Makoto Suzuki, who was signed by the Seattle Mariners; Masato Yoshii, a starting pitcher for the New York Mets; and Hideki Irabu, who signed with the Yankees and helped the team win a world championship in 1998.

Hideki Irabu was involved in another historic first. On May 7, 1999, he outdueled fellow Japanese national Mac Suzuki, not in the pro leagues of Japan but right on the legendary mound at Yankee Stadium. Their encounter was the first matchup of Japanese starting pitchers in American major-league history. The game was a win-win for Japanese ballplayers trying to prove their worth on a big-league stage. In 2001, the sensation of the Seattle Mariners was Ichiro Suzuki, the first all-star position player from Japan. That same year, the New York Mets also started Tsuyoshi Shinjo at right field. Players in Japan have worked hard over many years to elevate the status and competitive nature of Japanese baseball. These players are prime evidence that the talent pool is expanding quickly on a major-league level across the Pacific. What is more, they are challenging the adage that "history does not change, only the names do." Going back one hundred years, it would have been impossible for Issei to cross over into the major leagues. Today, the Japanese are welcomed with open arms. As long as they can contribute to the success of their teams, their ethnicity or religious backgrounds do not matter. All that matters is talent and heart.

ICHIRO SUZUKI

After leaving a nine-year Hall of Fame career with the Orix Blue Wave team in Japan's Nippon Professional Baseball, Ichiro joined Major League Baseball's Seattle Mariners. The first Japanese-born position player in the American League, Ichiro led the American League in batting average and stolen bases, in addition to being named the league's Rookie of the Year and Most Valuable Player. He has the major-league record for hits in a single season, with 262; won the Gold Glove Award in each of his first ten years in the major leagues; was named an All-Star ten times; and won the 2007 All-Star Game MVP award after a three-hit performance that included the game's first—and only—inside-the-park home run. Ichiro had ten consecutive two-hundred-hit seasons, the longest streak by any player, surpassing the Negro League All-Star Wee Willie Keeler's streak of eight. In his rookie season, he won the James "Cool Papa" Bell Legacy Award from the Negro League Baseball Museum for leading the American League in stolen bases. In the World Baseball Classic, Japan won the championship twice in a row, with Ichiro getting the game-winning hit in 2009. Ichiro is on track to become a Hall of Fame baseball player in two countries. His "Bushido" mentality both on and off the field is legendary. In every arena of human endeavor, there are icons of skill and artistry—Rudolf Nureyev in dance, Bruce Lee in martial arts and Ichiro Suzuki in baseball. Ichiro is a Blue Wave, a Mariner, a two-time WBC Champion, a Yankee and a Hall of Famer, but he will always be a samurai.

This "bridge across the Pacific" now flows freely. In 2003, Shigetoshi Hasegawa (Mariners), Hideki Matsui (Yankees) and Ichiro Suzuki (Mariners) all represented their teams in the All-Star Game for the American League. Hideki Matsui was an All-Star and MVP with the New York Yankees, and Daisuke Matsuzaka helped his Boston Red Sox win a World Series, much like Junichi Tazawa and Koji Uehara did in the 2013 championship season. Yu Darvish was the MVP pitcher in the 2009 for Japan in the World Baseball Classic and an All-Star for the Texas Rangers. His teammate Kazuo Matsui played with the Mets, Rockies and Astros. Hiroki Kuroda, Masahiro Tanaka and Ichiro Suzuki wear the Yankee pinstripes together. Norichika Aoki is with Kansas City, Kyuji Fujikawa and Darwin Barney of the Cubs arrived after Kosuke Fukudome and Hisashi Iwakuma pitches with the Mariners, following Kenji Johjima and Kazuhiro Sasaki. These players and more had the courage and tenacity to leave the comforts of family and friends and challenge themselves to the cultural changes in America and major-league baseball. The fans and communities in Japan might be losing their superstars to the majors, but with such strong youth teams and high school and college all-stars moving up to professional baseball, they simply reload with these new future baseball greats.

ACROSS THE GENERATIONS

For the first half of this century, Japanese Americans had leagues of their own—not by choice but because, like their colleagues in the Negro Leagues and the All-American Girls Leagues, Issei ballplayers were shut out of organized baseball. Yet baseball remained an anchor for Japanese immigrants and their U.S.-born descendants. Today, Nisei, Sansei and

Actor Pat Morita, Cappy Harada and Anaheim Angels pitcher Shigetoshi Hasegawa join in recognizing all of the Nisei players who contributed to building a bridge of goodwill across the Pacific. *Courtesy Kaz Arai.*

Yonsei are stepping up to the plate in a variety of capacities in baseball and in society around the globe.

Still-active Nisei continue to make their mark in coaching and administrative capacities, including Fibber Hirayama, the coach and scout at the Hiroshima Carp Baseball Academy in the Dominican Republic. Fibber says, "Baseball has been one of those elements that allowed me to develop as a person and an individual—plus it gave me opportunities." Another renowned Nisei, Howard Zenimura, is president of the Greater Boys' Baseball Club and tours with his USA baseball team to Japan and other countries, much as his father did in the 1920s and 1930s.

Eighty-eight-year-old Nisei Harry Shironaka is the captain of the Kids and Kubs softball team in Fort Lauderdale, Florida. A prewar Nisei all-star with the Walnut Grove Deltans, Harry competed with Joe and Dom DiMaggio when they toured with the San Francisco Seals. He still plays the game along with his wife of almost sixty years, Kimi, who is the Kubs' official batgirl.

Passing the torch. Masanori Murakami, a pitching instructor for the San Francisco Giants, works on some of the finer points of pitching with Yonsei Kurt Takahashi at a rookie camp in Scottsdale, Arizona, in 1996. *Courtesy Kaz Arai.*

Colleague and collaborator Fibber Hirayama coached and scouted at the Carp Baseball Academy in the Dominican Republic. *Courtesy Kaz Arai.*

Meanwhile, members of the youngest Japanese American generation to come of age are taking their place in the limelight. Scattered around Division I campuses playing baseball and headed for pro careers are such promising young athletes as Kevin Okimoto at Santa Clara, Scott Nakagawa at Washington State, Jon Asahina at LSU and Garret Shitanishi at the University of Nevada–Las Vegas.

On May 31, 1999, Kelly Inouye Perez helped her UCLA teammates win the NCAA Women's College World Series by beating Washington State 3–2. Other female players having an impact include Megumi Takasaka at U.C. Berkeley, Lisa Hashimoto at Utah, Stacy Kunishige at Fresno State and many other Sansei and Yonsei women in collegiate softball programs around the nation.

The current wave of Nikkei (all-generation) athletes, players and coaches represents the far-reaching story of the gradual recognition and acceptance of Japanese Americans. It is also a tribute to a one-hundred-year legacy of passion, pride and commitment to the all-American pastime that has been so deeply ingrained in Japanese American history and culture. Today's Sansei, Yonsei, Shin Issei and Japanese national players were handed the torch and are keeping alive the flame of passion that lit the way for Issei and Nisei ballplayers. As they make their way through the college and professional ranks, they are showing the way for future generations. Each succeeding generation becomes stronger, faster and bigger, and each brings its own style to the grand old game. All will be remembered for their pride in their culture and their legacy as pioneers in the story of a great American odyssey.

George "Doc" Omachi

George Hatsuo Omachi was born in San Fernando, California, and grew up in nearby Canoga Park. Sandlot baseball was a favorite pastime until organized ball came along in the 1930s with the upstart Japanese Athletic Union in Southern California. In 1942, his family moved to Fresno, California. His entire family became internees at the Fresno fairgrounds before being relocated to Jerome, Arkansas. George became active as a player with the Jerome All-Stars, which competed against and beat such teams as Arkansas A&M, the 442nd Regimental Combat team,

George Omachi. *Courtesy* Fresno Bee.

Hawaiian Asahi and other semipro teams.

During the times of internment, the government allowed internees who had jobs or families in the East or Midwest to leave the detention camps. In 1943, George and his wife, Alice, left Jerome to live in St. Louis, Missouri. George worked for a defense contractor building machine gun turrets and coached a local semipro municipal baseball team in Maplewood. In the latter capacity, he met Billy Southworth, the manager of the St. Louis Cardinals and, later, the Boston Braves. George absorbed all the major-league experience he encountered as an aide to Southworth.

In 1946, George returned to Fresno with his family. He began playing again with the Fresno Nisei team and served as an instructional coach with the Fresno Yellow Jackets, an all-black squad. As a result of his major league–caliber coaching expertise, he began managing and coaching the Fresno Nisei in 1955 after legendary coach Kenichi Zenimura retired. In 1961 and 1962, the Fresno Nisei were repeat winners as state champions as well as having been league champs five years in a row.

In 1968, George joined the New York Mets as their Central California scout. At various times, he also worked for the San Francisco Giants, Pittsburgh Pirates, Milwaukee Brewers and Houston Astros. In the early 1970s, the diminishing number of Sansei ballplayers prompted George to

Top: Former San Francisco Giant Will Clark and George Omachi, who served as a mentor to many players. *George Omachi collection*.

Left: Bobby Cox, manager of the World Series–winning Atlanta Braves, played second base in a Nisei tournament for George in Fresno. *Courtesy Atlanta Braves*.

Hall of Famer Tom Seaver competed and teamed up with the Nisei ballplayers in the Fresno area. *Courtesy Tom Seaver.*

form the Omachi All-Stars, a team of players of all races who were the cream of the crop of the entire Fresno County area.

Omachi's analytical approach and passion for the game were unparalleled. The Houston Astros organization referred to George as "the Doctor." As a scout, he would strip a potential major leaguer down to his shorts and study his form, paying special attention to muscle groups and mechanics. He was the only scout who could be trusted to make verbal recommendations about players and not file written reports. Any player having problems offensively or defensively, regardless of age, received special attention at no cost from "Doc" Omachi. The only criteria were a willingness to learn and a passion for the game. Among his major-league protégés are Tom Seaver, Bobby Cox, Rex Hudler and All-Star Geoff Jenkins.

TRAVIS TAKASHI ISHIKAWA

Travis Ishikawa earned a World Series title as first baseman for the 2010 San Francisco Giants. He had a pinch-hit double against the Texas Rangers' Mark Lowe in Game 1 of the series as the Giants won 11–7. In Game 4, he got his first start of the postseason, playing first base in the Giants' 4–0 victory. Ishikawa was drafted straight out of high school in 2002 by the San Francisco Giants. He made his major-league debut with the Giants in 2006. Since then, he has also played for the Milwaukee Brewers, the

Baltimore Orioles, the Pittsburgh Pirates and the New York Yankees. Ishikawa's father is a Sansei (third-generation Japanese American), and his mother is European American. His grandparents were held at the Amachee, Colorado concentration camp during World War II. From the pain and tragedy of being hit by a pitch in the face in his first game with the San Jose Giants minor-league team, he met his future wife, Rochelle, a dental assistant. They now have a daughter, who was born on his birthday. Ishikawa's Christian motto is: "Faith will always be the biggest part of anything that happens."

Kurt Kiyoshi Suzuki

At California State University–Fullerton, Kurt Suzuki received the nickname "Kurt Clutch." He helped the team capture the 2004 College World Series championship, thanks to his two-out RBI single in the bottom of the seventh inning, giving the Titans a 3–2 win over the Texas Longhorns. He was also selected an All-American by *Baseball America* and *Collegiate Baseball*, and he won the Johnny Bench Award as the country's top collegiate catcher. That same year, Kurt was drafted by the Oakland Athletics. In 2007, he joined the major-league club and, three days later, made his debut as a pinch hitter. On July 17, 2007, pitcher Shane Komine got into the game as a relief pitcher in the eighth inning against the Texas Rangers with Suzuki doing the catching. This was a milestone event, as it became the first time in major-league history that there was a battery where both Japanese American players were from Hawaii. In 2010, Kurt signed an extension with the A's. In 2012, he was traded to the Washington Nationals, on their way to the playoffs. In 2013, he was traded back to the A's, and in December 2013, he signed with the Minnesota Twins. Kurt and his wife, Renee, have supported the recovery of former Titan teammate Jon Wilhite, who was severely injured in the car crash that killed pitching prospect Nick Adenhart.

Chapter 9
CELEBRATIONS AND REMEMBRANCES

To live by being in harmony with what surrounds you is to be reminded that every end is followed by a new beginning.
—Sadaharu Oh

A century after the birth of Japanese American baseball, the inspiring story of this unique social and cultural odyssey is being rediscovered. The Issei pioneers are long gone, and the numbers of pre–World War II semipro Nisei players are dwindling. For a fortunate few veterans of the prewar leagues and the internment camps, recognition has come in the form of celebrations and belated homages to the skilled and courageous athletes who once played in leagues of their own. As contemporary Japanese Americans rediscover their rich baseball heritage, memory serves to connect cultures and generations, helping to ensure that America's future will be infused with the legacy of the past.

MAJOR LEAGUE BASEBALL HONORS THE NISEI

It was billed as the Japanese American "Field of Dreams." On July 20, 1996, the San Francisco Giants were the first major-league baseball club to recognize prewar Nisei ballplayers. Addressing forty-nine living legends and a crowd of three thousand family and friends in a pregame tailgate

The first historic major-league tribute to Nisei baseball was conducted at Candlestick Park on July 20, 1996, by the San Francisco Giants. Forty-nine Nisei prewar players were honored. *Courtesy Kaz Arai.*

celebration, Paul Osaki, executive director of the Japanese Cultural and Community Center of Northern California, said, "It is a day long overdue, but fortunately it is not too late. You are our heroes…You are American heroes, and today we say thank you."

The event might have been fifty years in coming, but the belated recognition was received gratefully. On this special day, the aging players could stand in center field, smell the grass and, perhaps for the last time, hear the applause of the crowd. Former ballplayer Kelly Matsumura of Parlier, California, said simply, "Today is the greatest day of my life."

Theirs was also an acknowledgement that something more lasting than a day's tribute was needed to preserve the story of the Issei, the Nisei and their descendants. Pat Gallagher, vice-president of the Giants, announced that a letter was being sent to the National Baseball Hall of Fame and Museum in Cooperstown urging the creation of an exhibit memorializing Japanese American baseball. "The story of American baseball is incomplete," the letter said, "unless a permanent exhibit is included on the contributions that Japanese American baseball made to the game."

Major League Baseball and the Hall of Fame like to say that baseball is a game of dreams and memories, and certainly it was these ideals that brought the forty-nine aging ballplayers and their friends and families to the stadium to recognize their contributions to their culture. A famous line in the film *Field of Dreams* goes, "If you build it, they will come." But Japanese American ballplayers could perhaps relate even more to another line from the film: "Ease his pain." For it was the pain of lost dreams that these players suffered more than half a century earlier—not just childhood dreams of being a professional ballplayer some day but also the dream of what the game of baseball symbolized about being an American. It was a time that we often forget about, and if baseball is a game of American hopes, dreams and memories, then it should preserve the story of that time as an integral part of its saga.

Some of the honorees will say that they were neither heroes nor legends, that they played for the love of the game and to entertain the Issei. But heroic acts come in all shapes and sizes. Sometimes they come in the form of bringing a smile to a young boy's face, making a father and mother proud or making a bad situation a little bit more bearable. These survivors of the camps who cleared spaces in the desert and built grandstands for the fans were indeed American heroes. Standing on the field of a major-league stadium on their day of recognition, perhaps for a moment they could feel like heroes and feel, too, the presence of teammates who had passed on standing with them on their field of dreams.

On July 25, 1997, a second group of prewar players took their bows at Dodger Stadium in Los Angeles. Peter O'Malley and the Dodgers billed the event as a Celebration of Densetsu (Legends). On this day, thirteen players from Southern California were honored as pioneers of the Japanese American baseball leagues. These players played for the Los Angeles Nippon, the San Fernando Aces, the San Pedro Skippers and the Guadalupe Young Men's Buddhist Association. Two of them—Al Sako and Tom Tomiyama—were teammates in 1924 on a goodwill baseball tour to Japan. Now they were being reunited more than seventy years later. "I was lucky enough to be able to pitch and travel to Japan— plus I got to see my grandmother in Kyushu," the ninety-five-year-old Sako reminisced. As Sako approached home plate before the ceremony, he gazed across the infield carpet and asked, "Is that real grass?" Informed that it was, he remarked, "Well, no wonder they don't make errors. I wouldn't make any errors on this field. You should have seen the fields I played on!"

Sako's teammate in 1924, Tom Tomiyama, migrated to Los Angeles from Fresno in the 1920s and played with the famed L.A. Nippon. The Nippon were part of the Los Angeles County League and played other semipro

The 1997 Dodger tribute to Nisei pioneers. Former teammates Al Sako and Tom Tomiyama (front row) toured Japan as a righty-lefty pitching combination for the Fresno Athletic Club. *Courtesy Kaz Arai.*

merchant teams like the Tom Mix Wildcats, the Paramount Studios, the Knights of Columbus, the Hollywood Athletic Club, the San Clemente Dons, the Pacific Steamship Company and teams from the Spanish American leagues. "I was a strong hitter and pitched pretty good, too," Tomiyama, now ninety-three, recalled. Among the other players on the semipro integrated team were Andrew McGalliard, Red Frasier and Gordon Ford. After Ford's playing career was over, he umpired many Nisei games. He was reunited with his L.A. Nippon teammates at Dodger Stadium.

The famed San Fernando Aces were represented at the ceremony by Pete Mitsui, George Tamura and George Hatago. Tee and Jimmy Okura and Yukio Tatsumi represented the San Pedro Skippers, the kingpins of Southern California in the late 1930s. Also present was longtime Los Angeles resident Noboru Takaki, a star shortstop for the Delano Nisei in the 1930s. Representing the Santa Maria region were Cappy Harada, Masao Iriyama and George Aratani.

On August 30, 1997, the San Francisco Giants, in conjunction with the City of San Francisco, paid tribute to seven pioneers who helped pave the way for other Americans to succeed in professional baseball in Japan. Mayor Willie Brown declared the day "Bridge Across the Pacific Day." The honorees included Wally Yonamine, Fibber Hirayama, Harvey and Howard Zenimura, Ben Mitsuyoshi, Cappy Harada and, posthumously, Lefty O'Doul. Former Giant Terry Whitfield, who played professionally in Japan, said of Yonamine and the other pioneers, "Wally and these Nisei players were the Jackie Robinsons for their people. I just wanted to thank them for opening up the doors for me and other Americans to become successful in professional baseball in Japan."

On Tuesday, June 23, 1998, the Oakland A's joined in the celebrations by honoring thirteen prewar players from the East Bay. Club president Sandy Alderson presented the players with special plaques in a pregame ceremony. A ceremonial first pitch was thrown by both Olympic gold medalist Kristi Yamaguchi and ninety-three-year-old Shiz Kawamura before forty-five thousand fans. The oldest player present was ninety-seven-year-old Sai Towata. Other teams participating in similar tributes included the Anaheim Angels, New York Mets and Fresno Grizzlies.

In 2011, the Fresno Grizzlies (AAA affiliate of the San Francisco Giants and member of the Pacific Coast League) honored the 1927 Nisei Fresno Athletic Club and its tour to Japan by wearing throwback jerseys with the dual American and Japanese patch.

REDISCOVERING A HIDDEN LEGACY: THE "DIAMONDS IN THE ROUGH" EXHIBITION

On May 4, 1996, an exhibition called "Diamonds in the Rough" opened at the Fresno Art Museum. The exhibition was the first historical collection of artifacts, memorabilia and images depicting the hidden legacy of Japanese Americans in baseball. The presentation included a captivating mélange of prewar uniforms, baseball equipment, trophies, jewelry and memorabilia. A special section devoted to baseball behind barbed wire showcased a diorama model of Zenimura Field at Gila River. The multimedia exhibition also boasted an interactive website, a lesson plan for teachers, documentaries and videos and panels of historical photographs.

After showing in Fresno, "Diamonds in the Rough" traveled to the Japanese Cultural and Community Center of Northern California; the Oakland

Baseball's 1998 season started with the "Diamonds in the Rough: Japanese Americans in Baseball" exhibit at the National Baseball Hall of Fame and Museum at Cooperstown, New York. *Courtesy Milo Stewart Jr., Baseball Hall of Fame Library.*

Asian Cultural Center; the San Jose Resource Center; the National Japanese American Historical Society; the California State Capitol Museum; the Herbst Exhibition Hall; the National Baseball Hall of Fame and Museum; the Hall of Fame Museum in Phoenix, Arizona; the Portland Hall of Fame Museum; the University of San Francisco; the Four Rivers Cultural Center in Ontario, Oregon; the Japanese Baseball Hall of Fame in Tokyo; and the Japanese-American National Museum in Los Angeles. Showings are also scheduled for Hawaii; Sao Paulo, Brazil; and the Babe Ruth Museum in Baltimore, Maryland.

Throughout the national tours associated with the exhibit, the media have gravitated to this unique portrayal of a legacy that time forgot. "I had no idea that the history of Japanese American baseball started at the beginning of the century. You become jaded into thinking that your legacy started with the bombing of Pearl Harbor," said CNN producer Rusty Dornan.

The day after interviewing ninety-two-year-old Shiz Kawamura, a prewar ATK baseball player, CNN ran the story for global audiences. That same evening, Shiz's son called him from the Philippines. Said Shiz, "I haven't talked with him in a long time. But he saw me on the news story. I also got a postcard from my old girlfriend back in Ohio. I haven't seen her in a long time." Regardless of whom Shiz was more excited to talk about, his son or his old flame, individuals who had long since parted company had once again been reconnected through baseball.

What is it about this one-hundred-year history that brings CNN, *Sports Illustrated* and other news services to the "Diamonds in the Rough" exhibits around the country? Perhaps part of the answer is the parallel experience of many other immigrant groups in the United States. And perhaps partly it is the power of America's national pastime to forge connections among all of those who, whatever their differences, cherish the grand old game.

PIONEERING ARCHITECTS OF BASEBALL: CHIURA AND GYO OBATA

From starting the first organized Japanese American baseball team to building America's premier baseball stadiums, the Obata family legacy represents the continuity and impact of a one-hundred-year tradition. This tradition is experienced in many forms by many Japanese American families. Two generations of Obatas have contributed to this one-hundred-year legacy in profound ways. This tradition began with Chiura Obata, the founding pioneer of the Fuji Athletic Club in 1903, and continues with his son Gyo, who designs and builds the world's finest baseball stadiums.

The early passions of Chiura Obata—art and baseball—were handed down to his son. "I remember my father being very athletic," Gyo recalls. Chiura taught art at the University of California–Berkeley and took his son to college athletic events. Gyo remembers, "Dad loved the Giants and became one of their most devoted fans. He would be fishing, teaching or out at social events listening to the games." But he also took his son on camping trips to Yosemite for weeks at a time. Chiura would do watercolor paintings while his friend Ansel Adams photographed the park.

Gyo took these inspirations and transformed them into his own passion— architecture. But what he will most likely be remembered for is the creation of the parks where baseball is played. As the chairman of Hellmuth Obata and Kassabaum (HOK), one of America's largest architectural engineering and planning firms, Gyo is the design force behind HOK Sport. HOK has created some of the world's most recognizable baseball stadiums: Camden

Obata family in Japan. Chiura Obata (front row, second from right) and his son Gyo (front row, far right) represent two generations of the baseball dynamic in America. Chiura played in the early immigrant stadiums, and Gyo designs and builds the finest stadiums in the world. *Chiura Obata family collection.*

One of HOK Sport's architectural masterpieces, Pac Bell Park in San Francisco, opened in the spring of 2000. *Courtesy HOK Sport and Assassi Productions.*

Yards (Baltimore), Jacob's Field (Cleveland), Coors Field (Denver), Comerica Park (Detroit), Enron Field (Houston) and Pac Bell Park in San Francisco.

Pilgrimage to Gila River

If the late 1990s were a time of rediscovering and celebrating the legacy of prewar Japanese American baseball, then it was also a time of remembrance. Imagine the mixed emotions of former detention camp internees traveling down the Pearl Harbor Freeway to visit the site of the Gila River camp in the middle of the Pima Indian Reservation in Arizona. This scenario took place on April 17, 1997, on a pilgrimage to Gila River. Among those who participated were actor Pat Morita and his wife, Evelyn; Howard Zenimura; Kerry Yo Nakagawa; Rick Noguchi; Gary Otake; Kaz Arai; Mas Inoshita; Step Tomooka; Gan Hanada; the camera crew from Nippon Hoso Kyokai; and the tribal council of the Gila River Indian Community. For Howard Zenimura, it was a reunion almost sixty years later to see Step Tomooka, against whom he once competed on Zenimura Field.

Mas Inoshita, a volunteer caretaker of the Butte Memorial site, unofficially adopted into the Pima Indian tribe, guided the group to the Gila River Indian Community Center. There they met with the Pima Indian governor, Mary Thomas. She is the spiritual leader of her people, and her positive magnetism filled the room as she greeted the former internees and their families.

Governor Thomas presented the group with gifts, including Gila River pendants, olive oil from Zenimura Field and bottled water. She explained how the Gila River Indian community is totally self-sufficient, deriving income from the Gila River Casino and Gila River Farms (olive oil, oranges, wheat, alfalfa), among other enterprises. The governor had just returned from Xian, China, and she described seeing an ancient hut that was exactly like those of the Pima Indians. The resemblance put a new spin on the ancient Asian migration to North America across the Bering Strait and fortified the theory of the spiritual kinship of Asian and North American cultures.

At one point, Governor Thomas asked Pat Morita and Howard Zenimura why they had made the journey to Gila River. She understood that Pat and Kenso were just teenagers when they had been in the camp. Pat acknowledged Kerry Nakagawa's insistence, good timing and a desire to reconnect with their past. Governor Thomas took their hands and began to cry. She said, "Babies were born on our sacred land, and some of your people died here. You are part of our community, and we apologize for what happened." Pat responded with great emotion that the Gila River Indians were not responsible for the internment of Japanese Americans and that the interns had been forced to live on their land. Governor Thomas, who was a child at the time of the internment, held feelings much like those of some of the Nisei. "We should have resisted the government's demands," she said. Tears flowed throughout the room like the ancient Gila River.

The group then trekked to the top of a hill to see the Butte Camp memorial. Permanent plaques dedicated to the internees and to Japanese American soldiers killed in action are anchored on the top of the hill. Miles and miles of foundations and overgrown weeds and sagebrush cover the camp landscape. Howard Zenimura went directly to his former barracks space and reflected on his stay. "We lived right here in apartment 13C," he said. "My mom, dad and brother Harvey stayed here. Next to us was my grandmother and her family." Pat and Howard stood in front of what used to be the mess hall. "Remember they used to ring the bell for us to come to eat?" said Pat.

A short distance from Block 28, Zenimura Field was now an olive orchard. Two mitts and a ball were provided so that Howard Zenimura and Pat could play catch again. What an incredible sight that was—Howard and Pat tossing the ball back and forth on Zenimura Field fifty-six years after they had played on the site as young internees. The moment brought images of desert sand and sagebrush transformed by community spirit, passion and labor to a field of dreams.

Almost sixty years later, the field has been transformed again, this time into a productive olive orchard. Down the road in Phoenix, another field of dreams has been constructed, this one to house the Arizona Diamondbacks. From sagebrush and sandlot baseball to major-league baseball, from barbed wire to olive branches and enterprising Pima Indians—these are the new relatives of Japanese Americans in Arizona.

Later that same evening, the roof of the $354 million Bank One Ballpark opened in preparation for a ball game. Behind home plate, Pat Morita belted out America's national anthem. Fifty thousand fans cheered his rendition.

THE ROAD TO COOPERSTOWN

On July 17, 1997, the California legislature approved Senate Concurrent Resolution 51 calling for a permanent exhibit of Japanese American baseball leagues in the National Baseball Hall of Fame and Museum in Cooperstown, New York. Sponsored by state senators Jim Costa and Patrick Johnston and assembly members Mike Honda and Nao Takasugi, the measure passed unanimously, 111–0. The resolution began by acknowledging baseball's status as America's national pastime and its rich store of legends, stories, history and culture. It then pointed out that, "although not widely known in this country until recent years," the Japanese American community had contributed a significant chapter to the history of baseball that paralleled "its rich contributions to the heritage of American society and the foundations on which this country stands."

The resolution went on to underscore the history of Japanese American baseball, citing the "love for the game" that led the Issei and Nisei to develop "an extensive, highly regarded network of separate Japanese American leagues throughout the U.S." that competed both in this country and abroad and "cemented and galvanized" communities throughout the nation. "In honor of their contribution to baseball," the resolution continued, "the Nisei baseball leagues should rightly have a permanent exhibit at the National Baseball Hall of Fame."

Sparked by the California legislation and by the support of major-league baseball executives Peter O'Malley (Los Angeles Dodgers), Larry Lucchino (San Diego Padres), Sandy Alderson (Oakland A's) and Patrick Gallagher (San Francisco Giants), the Hall granted temporary lodging for an exhibit called "Diamonds in the Rough: Japanese Americans in Baseball." In February 1998, a small band of aging former baseball players boarded a 767 airliner for the final stage of a lifelong odyssey. Over the intercom came the voice of the pilot, who announced, "Ladies and gentlemen, I'd like to welcome the Nisei baseball pioneers who are headed for the Hall of Fame in Cooperstown." Thunderous applause erupted for the delegation of heroes headed for their day of recognition. Hours later, a journey spanning three thousand miles and half a century ended for fifteen Nisei ballplayers as they entered the small village of Cooperstown.

The players walked through the entrance to the museum accompanied by a wave of children and grandchildren. As they took their walk of passage into the church-like building, reverently passing the images in the Hall of Fame gallery, they could feel the spirits of Jackie Robinson and other heroes greeting them.

On February 17, 1998, Nisei ballplayers from around the nation were recognized for their contribution to the American pastime at the Baseball Hall of Fame and Museum in Cooperstown, New York. *Courtesy Julie Lewis and the* Daily Star.

To visit baseball's mecca is to experience a treasure-trove of history. You marvel at the taped baseball that Babe Ruth made in reform school, Ty Cobb's sliding pads, Shoeless Joe Jackson's cleats, the bat that Roberto Clemente used to make his 3,000th and last hit, the ball that Mickey Mantle drove 565 feet...the treasures never end.

Among the hundreds of legends honored in the museum is Josh Gibson, the Negro Leagues star who was the only ballplayer ever to hit a ball out of Yankee Stadium. Josh and the other Negro Leagues greats are part of an exhibit entitled "Pride and Passion: The African American Baseball Experience." Turn the corner, and you encounter the All-American Girls story, a permanent exhibit that chronicles the history of the women's leagues. On the occasion of the Nisei players' visit, these stories of inclusion within the context of exclusion were complemented by the "Diamonds in the Rough" exhibit. What had begun as one family's exploration into a missing chapter in American baseball history had blossomed into a rich presentation housed in baseball's sacred ground for visitors from around the world to appreciate.

On February 17, 1998, the fifteen prewar Nisei players were the guests of honor at a packed dedication ceremony in the Hall's Grandstand Theater. All were at least eighty years old; one player, Harry Shirachi of Salinas, was ninety. Players representing both Southern and Northern California—and even Cheyenne, Wyoming—had made the trek to Cooperstown along with fifty relatives and friends from the West Coast. "My kids really wanted me to be here to represent all women who played," said Alice Hinaga Taketa, an all-star of the women's night leagues back in the 1930s. Shig Tokumoto of Hanford and Uncle Lefty Nishijima, who pitched against Jackie Robinson in 1937, were proud delegates from California's Central Valley.

All listened with pride as Hall of Fame president Donald C. Marr Jr. declared, "This incredibly dramatic exhibit gives baseball fans a wonderful opportunity to further their knowledge on an important aspect of baseball history." Frank Simio, vice-president of the Hall, spoke eloquently of history, culture and the compelling story of Americans keeping the national pastime alive, even behind barbed wire. Ted Spencer, the Hall's curator, told how he had enjoyed opening the crates for the exhibit along with Frank Simio and Donald Marr. "It was like Christmas again," Spencer related, "looking at the treasures of history. It is a compelling subject and an integral part of American culture that shows what lengths people went to play ball."

After the many organizations and people that helped to bring the exhibition to Cooperstown were acknowledged, it was time to honor players in the "Diamond Stadium in the Sky." The founding curator of the exhibit, Kerry Yo Nakagawa, talked about his father, who once pitched a complete-game no-hitter in eighth grade but never got to proudly wear a Nisei uniform because he was too busy working to keep the family farm going. The curator added that he never felt his father's presence more than he did that day in the Grandstand Theater. "Well Dad," he said, "you made it to the Hall of Fame with me."

For the Nisei players, the magical day in Cooperstown seemed to turn back the clock. Dressed in their uniforms, they had the effervescent energy of Little Leaguers. As they headed for the bus outside the museum after the ceremony, a light snow started to fall. It indeed felt like Christmas. A very special present had been given not only to the players but to all who care about Japanese American culture and history.

DIPLOMACY AND DIAMONDS IN THE JAPANESE HALL OF FAME

In November 1999, a motor coach of Nisei baseball pioneers approached the majestic Tokyo Dome. Inside the "Big Egg" was Japan's mecca of baseball museums, the Japanese Hall of Fame. Inside the Hall of Fame Gallery, looking down from the walls, were the bronze immortal faces of Japan's professional baseball legends. Enshrined there were three American Nisei ballplayers: Bozo Wakabayashi, Hisashi Koshimoto and Wally Yonamine. Bozo Wakabayashi was a legendary pitcher from Hawaii and a veteran of the Hanshin Tigers, Hisashi Koshimoto was prewar manager of the 1926 Mejii University baseball club and Wally Yonamine had been with the Yomiuri Giants.

A sea of bodies parted as the former U.S. Speaker of the House, Ambassador to Japan Thomas S. Foley, took his seat. The Japanese commissioner of professional baseball, Hiromori Kawashima, welcomed

In 1999, the "Diamonds in the Rough" exhibit traveled to the Japanese Baseball Hall of Fame in Tokyo, transforming it into a truly international experience. *Courtesy Miwako Atarashi.*

the honored guests, media and especially the fourteen Nisei ballplayers. Ambassador Foley said, "Thanks to the pioneering efforts of these players present and in spirit who are commemorated in this exhibition, they have helped to bring our two great nations closer together through sports."

Nisei pioneer Harry Shirachi, Hall of Famer Wally Yonamine and Commissioner Hiromori Kawashima officially cut the symbolic ribbon to open the exhibit. "Diamonds in the Rough: Japanese Americans in Baseball" had bridged the Pacific again and offered Japan a cultural gift on its national holiday.

LOOKING TO THE FUTURE

As we approach a new millennium, an inspiring resurgence of interest in Japanese American baseball "roots" has begun. A missing chapter in American baseball history has been unearthed that is a significant part of the culture and heritage ingrained into Japanese American society. Intergenerational dialogue throughout Nikkei communities across the country has resulted in a new era of ethnic pride. To the popular images of prewar Nisei pioneers as dirt farmers, gardeners or fishermen can now be added the proud image of a world-class baseball player.

As actor Pat Morita says, "Issei, Nisei, Sansei, Yonsei…if we do not record all this baseball history, it will be No-sei." With the renewed interest in Japanese American baseball history, many families are looking again at ancient scrapbooks and searching attics and garages for worn jerseys and long-forgotten artifacts. The old days of the sandlots and community ballparks live again in retellings for grandchildren and great-grandchildren to hear. The painful wartime memories remain buried, but the best times of the lives of the Nisei are resurrected and relived.

The old days also live again in the new teams and leagues that have sprouted throughout Hawaii and California. In Hawaii, the birthplace of this century-old legacy, the AJA (Americans of Japanese Ancestry) leagues are the home of new semipro powerhouses. On the mainland, the Japanese Athletic Union (JAU) in Southern California is gaining momentum every year. Sansei players are turning to coaching and handing the torch to the Yonsei athletes now climbing the ranks. Friendships based on a shared ethnic and cultural background mirror the golden years of the Issei and Nisei. These teams and organizations are the "ties that bind" in the

From Yukio Tatsumi (left), former Nisei player for the San Pedro Skippers, to Hideo Nomo (right), Rookie of the Year in 1995, the contribution of Japanese Americans and Japanese ballplayers has created the potential for young players like Kale Nakagawa to pursue professional careers in baseball. *Courtesy Alan Miyatake.*

Japanese American experience even as the subculture diversifies through interracial families.

From the early days of playing in segregated leagues to their more recent roles as promoters and ambassadors of baseball, Japanese American ballplayers demonstrated the ability to overcome adversity and make the most of opportunities in even the most difficult of circumstances. These proud Americans reinforce the saying, "Hope springs eternal."

Today, the future of Japanese American baseball looks bright. Japanese Americans have conquered every level of baseball in the high schools, colleges, minor leagues and, increasingly, the major leagues as well. Two goals that remain are to see a Japanese American Hall of Famer enshrined in Cooperstown and, sooner than that, a permanent exhibit in the Hall's museum on the one-hundred-year legacy of Japanese American baseball.

Japanese Hall of Famer Sadaharu Oh, the Yomiuri Giant legend who holds the world record for home runs with 868, has captured the universal spirit of all Nikkei ballplayers in these words:

My opponents lifted my spirits and, in doing so, reminded me of something that I had spent twenty-two years learning: that opponents and I were really one. My strength and skills were only half of the equation. The other half was theirs…I learned in fact there were no enemies. An opponent was someone whose strength joined to yours and created a certain result. Let someone call you enemy and attack you, and in that moment they lose the contest…My baseball career was a long, long initiation into a single secret: that at the heart of all things is love. We are, each of us, one with the universe that surrounds us—in harmony with it, not in conspiracy against it. To live by being in harmony with what surrounds you is to be reminded that every end is followed by a new beginning—and that the humblest of life's offerings is as treasured as the greatest in the eyes of the Creator.

The Issei and Nisei generations realized this spirit of *gambatte* (hard work, resilience and harmony) and tried to impart their wisdom to the younger generations, hoping that their descendants would never forget what the Issei and Nisei did to make their world a better place in which to live. By keeping the stories alive, we acknowledge these baseball pioneers and enrich our understanding of the Japanese American community's pride and passion, as well as its contribution to the diverse cultural heritage of America. In so doing, we see through a diamond that the best testimony to the greatness of this country can be found in the loyalty, love and sacrifice that it has inspired in its people.

Chapter 10
EXTRA INNINGS

AUTHORS

Since the 2001 release of the book *Through a Diamond: 100 Years of Japanese American Baseball*, many new exciting and magnificent writers have stepped up with their words of passion. My friend and "fantasy baseball" teammate Bill "Five for Five" Staples helped me win my first pitching shutout for the Baltimore Orioles team. Our coaches were Hall of Famers Brooks and Frank Robinson. Receiving the signed MVP award from Brooks (also know as the "Human Vacuum Cleaner") was one of the highlights of my baseball career. Bill joined our nonprofit NBRP (Nisei Baseball Research Project) as a director, webmaster and researcher. He recently wrote the biography of Kenichi Zenimura, entitled *Kenichi Zenimura: Japanese American Baseball Pioneer*, and won the 2011 SABR (Society of American Baseball Research) Award. His expertise and knowledge on the African American and Japanese American baseball dynamic is astounding. Kathryn Fitzmaurice was inspired to write her book *A Diamond in the Desert* based on her student Danley Shimasaki's diorama and report of the Gila River concentration camp. Danley's grandfather Sho scored the winning run against the Tucson Badgers in an 11–10 game. The book won the Bank Street Best Book award for 2013. One of the major characters in Fitzmaurice's book is my friend Tets "Natto" Furukawa, who was the starting pitcher for the Gila River Eagles and is a "living treasure" to this time period. *Barbed Wire Baseball*, written by Marissa Moss and illustrated by Yuko Shimizu, is the mesmerizing and touching true story of Kenichi Zenimura and his family behind barbed wire. It won the Junior Library Guild Selection award in 2013. Professor Samuel O. Regalado is a historian on Latino and Japanese American baseball. His recent book, *Nikkei Baseball: Japanese American Players from Immigration and Internment to the Major Leagues*, is a fascinating study of these time periods. *The Golden Game: The Story of California Baseball* by Kevin Nelson is the story of California baseball told through the refreshing prism of many diverse races. Jay Feldman once again triumphs with his exposé of a love story and relationships inside a Japanese American concentration camp entitled *Suitcase Sefton and the American Dream*. All of these writers are to be commended for taking on subject matter that is still such an obscure topic in America.

DIAMONDS IN THE ROUGH: ZENI AND THE LEGACY OF JAPANESE AMERICAN BASEBALL

This documentary, a 2001 finalist at the Palm Springs International Film Festival, features Noriyuki "Pat" Morita as narrator, on-camera host and co-writer. It is an exposé featuring Nisei legends Kenichi Zenimura and Wally Yonamine and many other Nisei baseball pioneers.

BASEBALL RELIQUARY

In 2006, Kenichi Zenimura was inducted into the Baseball Reliquary, otherwise known as the "West Coast Hall of Fame." Founded by Terry Cannon, it is a shrine of the eternals that elects its individuals on merits rather than statistics and playing ability, placing more importance on the imprint left by the individual on the baseball landscape though culture, humanity and education. Josh Gibson and Fernando Valenzuela were also inducted in 2006.

AMERICAN PASTIME

The movie culminates in a game, as it must, and it's obvious, too, who wins: the Americans.
—*Bruce Wallace,* Los Angeles Times

This award-winning dramatic narrative won the Audience Choice award at the 2007 International Asian American Film Festival in San Francisco. It tells the story of jazz music, baseball and a love story inside a Topaz, Utah concentration camp—along with the irony of the men who volunteered to fight for our country while their families were being imprisoned. It was a five-year dream film for the talented cast and crew members who united to tell the gripping and moving story of camp life for the eight thousand Nisei internees primarily from San Francisco. Today, the film and specific curriculum continues to educate and inspire students and teachers in Las Vegas, Arizona, San Jose, Fresno and Los Angeles, and screenings have been held from everywhere from the Smithsonian in Washington, D.C., to San Quentin Prison. Gary Mukai, director of SPICE (Stanford Program on International and Cross-Cultural Education), developed our two curriculums pro-bono to engage our teachers and students around the nation.

RUTH, GEHRIG AND NISEI BALLPLAYERS

Rare home movie footage on sixteen millimeter film from the Toshiyuki family to the Zenimura family uncovers twenty-one seconds of footage of Babe Ruth, Lou Gehrig and Nisei legends coming together for a group photo opportunity on October 29, 1927. Lou Gehrig and his Nisei teammates beat Babe Ruth's team 13–3 that day at Fireman's Ballpark in Fresno, California.

Fiftieth Golden Anniversary of Masanori Murakami

In 1964, Masanori "Mashi" Murakami signed with and played for the San Francisco Giants. Fifty years later, he is standing on the shoulders of so many Japanese players who have raised the major-league bar up even higher with their abilities, passion and dedication. On May 15, 2014, the San Francisco Giants paid tribute to the man who has risen to the occasion for his country and family. To honor my uncle Johnny and his Nisei teammates, I wore the 1927 Fresno Athletic Club uniform as Mashi's catcher for his first-pitch ceremony. I gave him the fastball sign, and he threw me a strike in front of forty thousand fans!

Appendix

A TIMELINE OF ASIAN AMERICAN BASEBALL

By Bill Staples, Nisei Baseball Research Project

1872: Baseball is introduced in Japan by American schoolteacher Horace Wilson. By the end of the century, it becomes Japan's most popular team sport.

1878: Shiki Masaoka organizes the first baseball club in Japan, the Shimbashi Athletic Club.

1897: Cleveland Spiders manager Oliver "Patsy" Tebeau attempts to sign a Japanese outfielder known in the press only as the "half-brother of Japanese wrestler Matsuda Shorakichi." The status of the Japanese outfielder's signing is never reported.

1899: The first recorded Japanese American baseball team—soon to be renamed the Excelsiors—is formed in Hawaii by Reverend Takie Okumura. Baseball in Hawaii quickly explodes in popularity, with organized leagues flourishing by the early 1900s.

1903: The First Japanese American baseball team on the mainland, the Fuji Athletic Club, is founded by Chiura Obata in San Francisco.

1905: Steere Noda organizes the Hawaiian Japanese American team, the Hawaiian Asahi, which became one of the most prolific teams west of the Rockies.

1905: The Waseda University baseball team arrives in San Francisco to begin the first in a series of baseball exchanges with American universities.

1905: New York Giants manager John McGraw invites Japanese outfielder Shumza Sugimoto to try out for the team in Hot Springs, Arkansas. The press acknowledges "the color line" potentially drawn against Sugimoto, so he chooses to play for the semi-pro New Orleans Creoles in Louisiana.

1906: Several players from Waseda join the Green Japanese of Nebraska, a barnstorming team in the Midwest, becoming the first professional baseball players of Japanese ancestry in the United States.

1907: The Hawaiian St. Louis team becomes the first foreign team to play ball in Japan. Keio University is their host team.

1913: The Alameda Taiiku-Kai semipro team is formed.

1913: The all-black Twenty-fifth Infantry is stationed at Schofield Barracks in Honolulu and begins competing against the island's top Japanese and Chinese ball clubs.

1913: The "Chinese University" ball club, a squad composed of Chinese and Japanese players from Honolulu, barnstorms the United States and finishes the tour with 120 wins and 20 loses.

1914: The Asahi Club from Seattle becomes the first Nisei baseball team to play baseball in Japan.

1914: The Florin Athletic Club is formed. A steady flow of teams travel to Japan (including Nisei teams), and Japanese university teams regularly travel to the United States. Waseda outfielder Goro Mikami joins J.L. Wilkinsen's "All-Nations" barnstorming club.

1915: The Hawaiian Asahi embark on a tour competing with teams from Japan, Korea and China.

1915–17: Japanese American baseball teams are forming on the mainland.

1916: Andy Yamashiro passes as Chinese and plays under the name Andy Yim.

1919: The Fresno Athletic Club is organized.

1920: The Stockton Yamato Athletic Club is organized.

1920: Kenichi Zenimura leaves Hawaii for the U.S. mainland.

1920s: During this decade, the Northern California Japanese baseball league forms semipro teams, and many semiprofessional "A" teams are established. This decade also sees the formation of teams for Japanese American women, who also make their mark on the diamond.

1923: Kenichi Zenimura recruits the top players from Hawaii and encourages them to settle in cities throughout Central California to help boost the level of competition for Japanese American baseball leagues.

1924: The Fresno Athletic Club makes its first tour to Japan.

1925: The Hawaiian Baseball League (HBL) forms.

1927: The Aratani company team, the Guadalupe Packers, is sent on a goodwill tour to Japan. The Fresno Athletic Club and the Philadelphia Royal Giants (all-stars of the Negro Leagues) compete in Japan for a mythical championship. On a barnstorming tour following their World Series victory, Babe Ruth and Lou Gehrig play an exhibition game in

Fresno that features Nisei all-stars Johnny Nakagawa, Kenichi Zenimura, Fred Yoshikawa and Harvey Iwata.

1928: Bozo Wakabayashi joins an all-Nisei team from Stockton en route to a goodwill tour in Japan. As a result, he stays in Japan to attend school and becomes a professional player for the Osaka Tigers.

1930s: The golden age of Nisei baseball continues as the Japanese Athletic Union is founded and important teams such as the San Fernando Nippon (later renamed the Aces) and the Nisei Athletic Club in Oregon are formed.

1932: Kenso Nushida becomes the first Japanese American to play professional baseball in the United States above the "D" level when he signs with the Pacific Coast League Sacramento Solons (Senators).

1934: Matsutaro Shoriki forms Japan's first pro team, the Yomiuri Shimbun Professional Baseball Team.

1934: Babe Ruth arrives in Japan for an eighteen-game barnstorming tour.

1935: After a suggestion from Lefty O'Doul, Shoriki renames his professional team the Tokyo Giants. The Giants make their first tour to the United States to play semipro and professional teams.

1937: The Alameda Kono all-star team makes its last tour to Japan, Korea, Manchuria and Harbin, Russia.

1942: More than 120,000 Americans of Japanese descent are relocated into detention camps and immediately form assembly center teams. Later in the year, when assembly center internees are reassigned to permanent camps, the first thing they do is build baseball diamonds and form teams.

1943: Kay Kiyokawa becomes the starting pitcher for the University of Connecticut. Jack Kakuuchi plays third base and gets two hits for the Camp Grant military team that defeats the Chicago Cubs' starting lineup.

1945–55: After the war, many new leagues and teams are formed, including the Little Tokyo Giants, the L.A. Tigers, the Nichiren Orions, the Stockton Asahi, the San Francisco Traders and the Sacramento All-Stars.

1947: Jackie Robinson breaks the color barrier and joins the Brooklyn Dodgers.

1949: Lefty O'Doul's San Francisco Seals of the Pacific Coast League arrive in Japan for a ten-game series.

1949: A game marks the appearance of the first all-Nisei battery in U.S. professional history when Jiro Nakamura and Hank Matsubu signed contracts with the Modesto Reds, a Pittsburg Pirates farm team.

1951: Wally Yonamine becomes the first foreigner to play professional ball in Japan when he signs with the Yomiuri Giants.

1952: Fibber Hirayama is signed by the Stockton Ports and plays for one year in the professional leagues. He plays ten years with the Hiroshima

Carp in Japan and later becomes a coach and scout for the team in the Dominican Republic.

1953–56: Major-league teams such as the New York Giants and Brooklyn Dodgers travel to Hawaii to play teams in the Hawaiian Baseball League.

1954: Joe DiMaggio and Marilyn Monroe arrive in Japan for their honeymoon and a series of batting clinics. Nisei Kenshi "Harvey" Zenimura serves as interpreter for DiMaggio and his Hiroshima Carp teammates.

1961: The Sacramento Solons of the Pacific Coast League are purchased by Nick Morgan, move to Honolulu and are renamed the Hawaiian Islanders. Over the years, they serve as a farm team for several major-league teams, including the Chicago White Sox, the Washington Senators and the San Diego Padres.

1964: Bozo Wakabayashi is the first American Nisei to be inducted into the Japanese Hall of Fame.

1965: Masanori Murakami becomes the first Japanese national to play in the major leagues when he signs with the San Francisco Giants.

1965: Frank and Henry Ota each captain the baseball team for their class at Dartmouth.

1967: Mike Lum, a Japanese American adopted and raised by Chinese American parents, joins the Atlanta Braves and becomes the first Japanese American to play in the majors.

1968: George Omachi joins the New York Mets as the team's California scout.

1974: Hawaiian Asahi upsets world champion Cuba in an exhibition game in Tokyo.

1975: Sansei Ryan Kurosaki signs with the St. Louis Cardinals and becomes the first Japanese American (with a Japanese American surname) to play in the major leagues.

1977: Lenn Sakata is called up to play with the Milwaukee Brewers and becomes the first Japanese American position player.

1983: Lenn Sakata becomes the first Japanese American to participate in a World Series game.

1991: Don Wakamatsu becomes the first Yonsei to play in the majors when he is called up to the Chicago White Sox.

1995: Hideo Nomo from Osaka is named National League Rookie of the Year with the Los Angeles Dodgers.

1996: The "Diamonds in the Rough" exhibit opens in Fresno, and the first major-league tribute to Nisei baseball is conducted at Candlestick Park by the San Francisco Giants.

1997: The Los Angeles Dodgers honor Nisei legends such as teammates Al Sako and Tom Tomiyama, who are reunited for the first time in seventy-five years.

1998: The National Baseball Hall of Fame at Cooperstown displays the "Diamonds in the Rough" exhibit and honors surviving Nisei baseball pioneers.

1998: Don Wakamatsu is named Class "A" Minor League Manager of the Year with the Diamondbacks organization.

1999: The Japanese Hall of Fame in Tokyo honors Nisei ballplayers with the opening of the "Diamonds in the Rough" exhibit at the Tokyo Dome.

2000: Hawaiian Onan Masaoka debuts with the Los Angeles Dodgers.

2001: The Ichiro era begins as he goes on to a Hall of Fame career in two countries.

2006: Kenichi Zenimura is elected into the Baseball Reliquary Shrine of the Eternals along with Fernando Valenzuela and Josh Gibson.

2007: Warner Brothers releases the major motion picture *American Pastime*, which details the importance of baseball to the Japanese American concentration camp experience.

2008: Don Wakamatsu is named the skipper of the Seattle Mariners and in doing so becomes the first Asian American manager in MLB history.

2009: Japan wins the World Baseball Classic for the second time in a row.

2010: Travis Ishikawa of the San Francisco Giants joins Lenn Sakata as the only other Japanese American ballplayer to play in and win a World Series. Ishikawa played in a total of ten games during the 2010 postseason, including one start at first base during Game 4 of the World Series. He finished two for ten at the plate with two runs, a double and an RBI.

2011: Darwin Barney (Japanese/Korean ancestry) earns a spot on the Chicago Cubs' Opening Day roster as the starting second baseman. After hitting .326 with fourteen RBIs in his first month, he was named the National League Rookie of the Month for April.

2012: Yu Darvish signs with the Texas Rangers after an all-star career in Japan with the Hokkaido Nippon Ham Fighters.

2014: Masahiro Tanaka signs with the New York Yankees for a seven-year, $155 million commitment after starring for the Tohoku Rakuten Golden Eagles in Nippon Professional Baseball's Pacific League.

SELECTED BIBLIOGRAPHY

BOOKS

Goto, Chimpei. *The Japanese Baseballdom of Hawaii*. Honolulu: Hojin Yakyushi Shuppankai, 1940.

Leutzinger, Richard. *Lefty O'Doul: The Legend That Baseball Nearly Forgot*. Carmel, CA: Carmel Bay Publishing Group, 1997.

Miike, Fred. *Baseball-Mad Japan*. Tokyo: self-published, 1932.

Nagata, Yoichi. *Jimmy Horio and U.S./Japan Baseball: A Social History of Baseball*. Los Angeles: Japanese American National Museum, 2000.

Niiya, Brian, ed. *Japanese American History: An A-to-Z Reference from 1868 to the Present*. Los Angeles: Japanese American National Museum, 1993.

———. *More Than a Game: Sport in the Japanese American Community*. Los Angeles: Japanese American National Museum, 2000.

Oh, Sadaharu, and David Falkner. *Sadaharu Oh: A Zen Way of Baseball*. New York: Vintage Books, 1985.

Okumara, Takie. *Seventy Years of Divine Blessings*. Honolulu: Makiki Christian Church, 1939.

Suehiro, Arthur. *Honolulu Stadium: Where Hawaii Played*. Honolulu: Watermark Publishing, 1995.

PERIODICALS

Davis, David. "A Field in the Desert That Felt Like Home." *Sports Illustrated*, November 1998, 37–39.

Feldman, Jay. "Baseball Behind Barbed Wire." *Whole Earth Review Magazine*, Winter 1990, 36–43.

Gleeson, Scoop. "Art Shafer Tells How He Coached the Members of Keio University Ball Team in the Inside Plays." *San Francisco Bulletin*, Summer 1911, C-1.

Harris, Mark. "An Outfielder for Hiroshima." *Sports Illustrated*, October 1958, 177–89.

Hendsch, David A. "A Photo, a Tour, a Life." *The National Pastime* 18 (Summer 1998): 82–84.

Henson, Steve. "Japanese American Carrying on a Long Tradition." *Los Angeles Times*, September 1997, A-20.

Kashiwagi, Soji. "Baseball Crazy." *Rafu Shimpo*, March 1999, 3.

Machado, Carl. "Hawaii's Nisei in Baseball." *Pacific Magazine*, Summer 1948, 20–21.

Ohira, Rod. "Pinstripes & Pride." *Honolulu Star Bulletin*, February 1998, A-8.

Wilson, Lyle K. "Harlem Globetrotters Baseball Team." *The National Pastime* 17 (Summer 1997): 80.

UNPUBLISHED MATERIAL

Cellino, Maria Elena. "U.S. on Trial." Film treatment. Inner Circle Productions, 1983.

Masaoka, Shiki. Translated by Royichi Suzuki from the Japanese article "Tanka Poems" by Nobuyuki Yuasa, University of Hiroshima, 1998.

Mullan, Michael L. "Ethnicity and Sport: The Wapato Nippons and Prewar Japanese American Baseball." Master's thesis, Swarthmore College, 1998.

Shibazaki, Royichi. "Seattle and the Japanese–United States Baseball Connection, 1905–1926." Master's thesis, University of Washington, 1981.

OTHER SOURCES

Baseball Hall of Fame and Museum. "Museum Guide." Tokyo, Summer 1998: 8–9.

Hendsch, David A. "Fresno Shows the Japanese How to Do It: Baseball in the Making." Twenty-eighth National Convention Brochure, Society of American Baseball Research, 1998: 28–30.

Mr. Baseball. "Alexander Cartwright." www.mrbaseball.com/cartwrighthistory.php.

Otake, Gary, and Rosalyn Tonai. "Nikkei Heritage." San Francisco: National Japanese American Historical Society, 1997.

Takasumi, Mas, and Homer Yasui. "History of the Nisei Athletic Club (NAC) of Hood River." Summer 1998.

Tworkov, Helen. "The Baseball Diamond Sutra." Cooperstown, NY: National Baseball Hall of Fame and Museum, 1939.

INTERVIEWS WITH THE AUTHOR

1983: Mas Yano

1985: Yoshino Hasegawa

1990: Hugo Nishimoto

1991: Bill Matsumoto

1994: Toshio Nakagawa, George Omachi

1996: Al Bier, Rusty Dornan, Pat Gallagher, Fibber Hirayama, Jiro Kanayama, Sayo Kubo, Kady Mimura, George Omachi, Paul Osaki, Jere Takahashi, Tom Tomyama, Jiggs Yamata, Sab Yamata, Howard Zenimura

1997: George Aratani, Gordon Ford, Urban Griff, Jack Hannah, Cappy Harada, Masao Hirata, Ted Hirayama, Harry Honda, Henry Honda, Tashi Hori, Kaz Ikeda, Lawson Inada, Mas Inoshita, Ryo Kashiwagi, George Kataoka, Shig Kawaii, Shiz Kawamura, Kay Kiyokawa, Noboru Kobayashi, Moon Kurima, Ryan Kurosaki, Tommy Lasorda, Harry Masato, Hank Matsubu, Kelly Matsumura, Norman Mineta, Pete Mitsui, Pat Morita, Lefty Nishijima, Henry Ota, Minol Ota, Lenn Sakata, Al Sako, Todd Shimamoto, Harry Shirachi, Kat Shitanishi, Takeo Suo, Jere Takahashi, Alice Hinaga Taketa, Dan Takeuchi, Shigeo Takeyama, Barry Tamura, George Tamura, Ed Tanaka, Yukio Tatsumi, Mary Thomas, Shig Tokumoto, Tom Tomyama, Step Tomooka, Bill Tsukamoto, Ted Tsuyuki, Babe Utsumi, Ken Wallenberg, Terry Whitfield, Lilian Yajima, Wally Yonemine, Ted Yoshiwara, Harvey Zenimura, Howard Zenimura

1998: George Aratani, Harry Honda, Herb Iseri, Davey Johnson, Erwin Raven, George Suzuki, Don Wakamatsu, Kiyoko Zenimura

1999: Harry Honda, Onan Masaoka, Gyo Obata

INDEX

ABOUT THE AUTHOR

While coaching his son's Little League baseball team in Fresno, California, Kerry Yo Nakagawa was initially inspired to embark on a personal exploration to preserve the legacy of Japanese American Baseball and culture for future generations of Japanese Americans. It evolved into a full-time nonprofit project, and the Nisei Baseball Research Project (NBRP) was born eighteen years ago.

Baseball, and sports in general, have been a large part of the Nakagawa legacy. In 1993, Kerry swam from Alcatraz prison to San Francisco, and in 1994, he played as an all-star for the national champion Fresno Bandit semipro team. He is also a black

Courtesy Ko Yang.

belt in the martial arts and an advanced tennis player. His athletic family history includes his dad, who was a semipro football player and sumo champion, and his uncles—Johnny, Lefty and Mas—who competed with Lou Gehrig, Babe Ruth, Lefty O'Doul, Jackie Robinson and the all-stars of the Negro League.

His dedication to the NBRP project is well respected and has morphed into a educational organization to bring awareness and education about

Japanese American concentration camps through the prism of baseball and its many multimedia projects. The NBRP exhibit "Diamonds in the Rough" has achieved international status and has been shown in such locations as the National Baseball Hall of Fame in Cooperstown and the Japanese Baseball Hall of Fame in Tokyo. Kerry's other visions to communicate this story include a documentary with Pat Morita entitled *Diamonds in the Rough: Zeni and the Legacy of Japanese American Baseball* and the Telly Award–winning educational documentary *Site to Patriotism*. He produced and acted in the award-winning film *American Pastime*, which is still educating and entertaining teachers and students through its dramatic narrative and specific curriculum. He is an author, filmmaker, actor, historian, husband and father of two spectacular professional kids.